MW01286615

GEORGIA EVIDENCE CODE
2019 Edition
Updated through January 1, 2019

Michigan Legal Publishing Ltd.
QUICK DESK REFERENCE SERIES™

Academic and bulk discounts available at
www.michlp.com

WE WELCOME YOUR FEEDBACK: info@michlp.com

ISBN-13: 978-1-64002-067-2

Table of Contents

CHAPTER 1. GENERAL PROVISIONS

ARTICLE 1. PURPOSE AND APPLICABILITY OF RULES OF EVIDENCE

§ 24-1-1. Purpose and construction of the rules of evidence

The object of all legal investigation is the discovery of truth. Rules of evidence shall be construed to secure fairness in administration, eliminate unjustifiable expense and delay, and promote the growth and development of the law of evidence to the end that the truth may be ascertained and proceedings justly determined.

§ 24-1-2. Applicability of the rules of evidence

(a) The rules of evidence shall apply in all trials by jury in any court in this state.

(b) The rules of evidence shall apply generally to all nonjury trials and other fact-finding proceedings of any court in this state subject to the limitations set forth in subsections (c) and (d) of this Code section.

(c) The rules of evidence, except those with respect to privileges, shall not apply in the following situations:

    (1) The determination of questions of fact preliminary to admissibility of evidence when the issue is to be determined by the court under Code Section 24-1-104;

    (2) Criminal proceedings before grand juries;

    (3) Proceedings for extradition or rendition;

    (4) Proceedings for revoking parole;

    (5) Proceedings for the issuance of warrants for arrest and search warrants except as provided by subsection (b) of Code Section 17-4-40;

    (6) Proceedings with respect to release on bond;

    (7) Dispositional hearings and custody hearings in juvenile court; or

    (8) Contempt proceedings in which the court, pursuant to subsection (a) of Code Section 15-1-4, may act summarily.

(d)

    (1) In criminal commitment or preliminary hearings in any court, the rules of evidence shall apply except that hearsay shall be admissible.

    (2) In in rem forfeiture proceedings, the rules of evidence shall apply except that hearsay shall be admissible in determining probable cause or reasonable cause.

    (3) In presentence hearings, the rules of evidence shall apply except that hearsay and character evidence shall be admissible.

    (4) In administrative hearings, the rules of evidence as applied in the trial of nonjury civil actions shall be followed, subject to special statutory rules or agency rules as authorized by law.

(e) Except as modified by statute, the common law as expounded by Georgia courts shall continue to be applied to the admission and exclusion of evidence and to procedures at trial.

ARTICLE 2. GENERAL EVIDENTIARY MATTERS

§ 24-1-103. Rulings on evidence

(a) Error shall not be predicated upon a ruling which admits or excludes evidence unless a substantial right of the party is affected and:

    (1) In case the ruling is one admitting evidence, a timely objection or motion to strike appears of record, stating the specific ground of objection, if the specific ground was not apparent from the context; or

    (2) In case the ruling is one excluding evidence, the substance of the evidence was made known to the court by an offer of proof or was apparent from the context within which questions were asked.

(b) Once the court makes a definitive ruling on the record admitting or excluding any evidence, either at or before trial, a party need not renew an objection or offer of proof to preserve such claim of error for appeal.

(c) The court shall accord the parties adequate opportunity to state grounds for objections and present offers of proof. The court may add any other or further statement which shows the character of the evidence, the form in which it was offered, the objection made, and the ruling thereon. The court may direct the making of an offer of proof in question and answer form.

(d) Jury proceedings shall be conducted, to the extent practicable, so as to prevent inadmissible evidence from being suggested to the jury by any means, including, but not limited to, making statements or offers of proof or asking questions in the hearing of the jury.

(e) Nothing in this Code section shall preclude a court from taking notice of plain errors affecting substantial rights although such errors were not brought to the attention of the court.

§ 24-1-104. Preliminary questions

(a) Preliminary questions concerning the qualification of a person to be a witness, the existence of a privilege, or the admissibility of evidence shall be determined by the court, subject to the provisions of subsection (b) of this Code section. In making its determination, the court shall not be bound by the rules of evidence except those with respect to privileges. Preliminary questions shall be resolved by a preponderance of the evidence standard.

(b) When the relevancy of evidence depends upon the fulfillment of a condition of fact, the court shall admit it upon, or subject to, the introduction of evidence sufficient to support a finding of the fulfillment of the condition.

(c) Hearings on the admissibility of confessions shall in all cases be conducted out of the hearing of the jury. Hearings on other preliminary matters shall be conducted out of the hearing of the jury when the interests of justice require or when an accused is a witness and requests a hearing outside the presence of the jury.

(d) The accused shall not, by testifying upon a preliminary matter, become subject to cross-examination as to other issues in the proceeding.

(e) This Code section shall not limit the right of a party to introduce before the jury evidence relevant to weight or credibility.

§ 24-1-105. Limited admissibility

When evidence which is admissible as to one party or for one purpose but which is not admissible as to another party or for another purpose is admitted, the court, upon request, shall restrict the evidence to its proper scope and instruct the jury accordingly.

§ 24-1-106. Introduction of remaining portions of writings or recorded statements

When a writing or recorded statement or part thereof is introduced by a party, an adverse party may require the introduction at that time of any other part or any other writing or recorded statement which, in fairness, should be considered contemporaneously with the writing or recorded statement.

CHAPTER 2. JUDICIAL NOTICE

ARTICLE 1. ADJUDICATIVE FACTS

§ 24-2-201. Judicial notice of adjudicative facts

(a) This Code section governs only judicial notice of adjudicative facts.

(b) A judicially noticed fact shall be a fact which is not subject to reasonable dispute in that it is either:
    (1) Generally known within the territorial jurisdiction of the court; or
    (2) Capable of accurate and ready determination by resort to sources whose accuracy cannot reasonably be questioned.

(c) A court may take judicial notice, whether or not requested by a party.

(d) A court shall take judicial notice if requested by a party and provided with the necessary information.

(e) A party shall be entitled, upon timely request, to an opportunity to be heard as to the propriety of taking judicial notice and the tenor of the matter noticed. In the absence of prior notification, such request may be made after judicial notice has been taken.

(f) Judicial notice may be taken at any stage of the proceeding.

(g)

(1) In a civil proceeding, the court shall instruct the jury to accept as conclusive any fact judicially noticed.

(2) In a criminal proceeding, the court shall instruct the jury that it may, but is not required to, accept as conclusive any fact judicially noticed.

ARTICLE 2. LEGISLATIVE FACTS; ORDINANCES OR RESOLUTIONS

§ 24-2-220. Judicial notice of legislative facts

The existence and territorial extent of states and their forms of government; all symbols of nationality; the laws of nations; all laws and resolutions of the General Assembly and the journals of each branch thereof as published by authority; the laws of the United States and of the several states thereof as published by authority; the uniform rules of the courts; the administrative rules and regulations filed with the Secretary of State pursuant to Code Section 50-13-6; the general customs of merchants; the admiralty and maritime courts of the world and their seals; the political makeup and history of this state and the federal government as well as the local divisions of this state; the seals of the several departments of the government of the United States and of the several states of the union; and all similar matters of legislative fact shall be judicially recognized without the introduction of proof. Judicial notice of adjudicative facts shall be governed by Code Section 24-2-201.

§ 24-2-221. Judicial notice of ordinance or resolution

When certified by a public officer, clerk, or keeper of county or municipal records in this state in a manner as specified for county records in Code Section 24-9-920 or in a manner as specified for municipal records in paragraph (1) or (2) of Code Section 24-9-902 and in the absence of contrary evidence, judicial notice may be taken of a certified copy of any ordinance or resolution included within a general codification required by paragraph (1) of subsection (b) of Code Section 36-80-19 as representing an ordinance or resolution duly approved by the governing authority and currently in force as presented. Any such certified copy shall be self-authenticating and shall be admissible as prima-facie proof of any such ordinance or resolution before any court or administrative body.

CHAPTER 3. PAROL EVIDENCE

§ 24-3-1. Parol evidence contradicting writing inadmissible generally

Parol contemporaneous evidence shall be generally inadmissible to contradict or vary the terms of a valid written instrument.

§ 24-3-2. Proof of unwritten portions of contract admissible where not inconsistent

If the writing does not purport to contain all the stipulations of the contract, parol evidence shall be admissible to prove other portions thereof not inconsistent with the writing; collateral undertakings between parties of the same part among themselves would not properly be looked for in the writing.

§ 24-3-3. Contemporaneous writings explaining each other; parol evidence explaining ambiguities

(a) All contemporaneous writings shall be admissible to explain each other.
(b) Parol evidence shall be admissible to explain all ambiguities, both latent and patent.

§ 24-3-4. Circumstances surrounding execution of contracts

The surrounding circumstances shall always be proper subjects of proof to aid in the construction of contracts.

§ 24-3-5. Known usage

Evidence of known and established usage shall be admissible to aid in the construction of contracts as well as to annex incidents.

§ 24-3-6. Rebuttal of equity; discharge of contract; proof of subsequent agreement; change of time or place of performance

Parol evidence shall be admissible to rebut an equity, to discharge an entire contract, to prove a new and distinct subsequent agreement, to enlarge the time of performance, or to change the place of performance.

§ 24-3-7. Proof of mistake in deed or written contract

Parol evidence shall be admissible to prove a mistake in a deed or any other contract required by law to be in writing.

§ 24-3-8. Original or subsequent voidness of writing

Parol evidence shall be admissible to show that a writing either was originally void or subsequently became void.

§ 24-3-9. Explanation or denial of receipts

Receipts for money shall always be only prima-facie evidence of payment and may be denied or explained by parol.

§ 24-3-10. Explanation of blank endorsements

Blank endorsements of negotiable paper may always be explained between the parties themselves or those taking with notice of dishonor or of the actual facts of such endorsements.

CHAPTER 4. RELEVANT EVIDENCE AND ITS LIMITS

§ 24-4-401. "Relevant evidence" defined

As used in this chapter, the term "relevant evidence" means evidence having any tendency to make the existence of any fact that is of consequence to the determination of the action more probable or less probable than it would be without the evidence.

§ 24-4-402. Relevant evidence generally admissible; irrelevant evidence not admissible

All relevant evidence shall be admissible, except as limited by constitutional requirements or as otherwise provided by law or by other rules, as prescribed pursuant to constitutional or statutory authority, applicable in the court in which the matter is pending. Evidence which is not relevant shall not be admissible.

§ 24-4-403. Exclusion of relevant evidence on the grounds of prejudice, confusion, or waste of time

Relevant evidence may be excluded if its probative value is substantially outweighed by the danger of unfair prejudice, confusion of the issues, or misleading the jury or by considerations of undue delay, waste of time, or needless presentation of cumulative evidence.

§ 24-4-404. Character evidence not admissible to prove conduct; exceptions; other crimes

(a) Evidence of a person's character or a trait of character shall not be admissible for the purpose of proving action in conformity therewith on a particular occasion, except for:
  (1) Evidence of a pertinent trait of character offered by an accused or by the prosecution to rebut the same; or if evidence of a trait of character of the alleged victim of the crime is offered by an accused and admitted under paragraph (2) of this subsection, evidence of the same trait of character of the accused offered by the prosecution;
  (2) Subject to the limitations imposed by Code Section 24-4-412, evidence of a pertinent trait of character of the alleged victim of the crime offered by an accused or by the prosecution to rebut the same; or evidence of a character trait of peacefulness of the alleged victim

offered by the prosecution in a homicide case to rebut evidence that the alleged victim was the first aggressor; or

(3) Evidence of the character of a witness, as provided in Code Sections 24-6-607, 24-6-608, and 24-6-609.

(b) Evidence of other crimes, wrongs, or acts shall not be admissible to prove the character of a person in order to show action in conformity therewith. It may, however, be admissible for other purposes, including, but not limited to, proof of motive, opportunity, intent, preparation, plan, knowledge, identity, or absence of mistake or accident. The prosecution in a criminal proceeding shall provide reasonable notice to the defense in advance of trial, unless pretrial notice is excused by the court upon good cause shown, of the general nature of any such evidence it intends to introduce at trial. Notice shall not be required when the evidence of prior crimes, wrongs, or acts is offered to prove the circumstances immediately surrounding the charged crime, motive, or prior difficulties between the accused and the alleged victim.

§ 24-4-405. Methods of proving character

(a) In all proceedings in which evidence of character or a trait of character of a person is admissible, proof shall be made by testimony as to reputation or by testimony in the form of an opinion.

(b) In proceedings in which character or a trait of character of a person is an essential element of a charge, claim, or defense or when an accused testifies to his or her own character, proof may also be made of specific instances of that person's conduct. The character of the accused, including specific instances of the accused's conduct, shall also be admissible in a presentencing hearing subject to the provisions of Code Section 17-10-2.

(c) On cross-examination, inquiry shall be allowable into relevant specific instances of conduct.

§ 24-4-406. Habit; routine practice

Evidence of the habit of a person or of the routine practice of an organization, whether corroborated or not and regardless of the presence of eyewitnesses, is relevant to prove that the conduct of the person or organization on a particular occasion was in conformity with such habit or routine practice.

§ 24-4-407. Subsequent remedial measures

In civil proceedings, when, after an injury or harm, remedial measures are taken to make such injury or harm less likely to recur, evidence of the remedial measures shall not be admissible to prove negligence or culpable conduct but may be admissible to prove product liability under subsection (b) or (c) of Code Section 51-1-11. The provisions of this Code section shall not require the exclusion of evidence of remedial measures when offered for impeachment or for another purpose, including, but not limited to, proving ownership, control, or feasibility of precautionary measures, if controverted.

§ 24-4-408. Compromises and offers to compromise

(a) Except as provided in Code Section 9-11-68, evidence of:
    (1) Furnishing, offering, or promising to furnish; or
    (2) Accepting, offering, or promising to accept
(b) a valuable consideration in compromising or attempting to compromise a claim which was disputed as to either validity or amount shall not be admissible to prove liability for or invalidity of any claim or its amount.
(c) Evidence of conduct or statements made in compromise negotiations or mediation shall not be admissible.
(d) This Code section shall not require the exclusion of any evidence otherwise discoverable merely because it is presented in the course of compromise negotiations or mediation. This Code section shall not require exclusion of evidence offered for another purpose, including, but not limited to, proving bias or prejudice of a witness, negating a contention of undue delay or abuse of process, or proving an effort to obstruct a criminal investigation or prosecution.

§ 24-4-409. Payment of medical and similar expenses

Evidence of furnishing, offering, or promising to pay medical, hospital, or similar expenses occasioned by an injury shall not be admissible to prove liability for the injury.

§ 24-4-410. Inadmissibility of pleas, plea discussions, and related statements

Except as otherwise provided by law, evidence of the following shall not, in any judicial or administrative proceeding, be admissible against the criminal defendant who made the plea or was a participant in the plea discussions:
    (1) A plea of guilty which was later withdrawn;
    (2) A plea of nolo contendere;
    (3) Any statement made in the course of any proceedings in which a guilty plea or a plea of nolo contendere was entered and was later withdrawn, vacated, or set aside; or
    (4) Any statement made in the course of plea discussions with an attorney for the prosecuting authority which does not result in a plea of guilty or which results in a plea of guilty later withdrawn, vacated, or set aside;
provided, however, that the statements described in paragraphs (1) through (4) of this Code section shall be admissible in any proceeding wherein another statement made in the course of the same plea or plea discussions has been introduced and the statement ought in fairness be considered contemporaneously with it or in a criminal proceeding for perjury or false

statement if the statement was made by the accused under oath, on the record, and in the presence of counsel or after the accused voluntarily waived his or her right to counsel.

§ 24-4-411. Liability insurance

In all civil proceedings involving a claim for damages, evidence that a person was or was not insured against liability shall not be admissible except as provided in this Code section. This Code section shall not require the exclusion of evidence of insurance against liability in proceedings under Code Section 40-1-112 or when such evidence is offered for a relevant purpose, including, but not limited to, proof of agency, ownership, or control, and the court finds that the danger of unfair prejudice is substantially outweighed by the probative value of the evidence.

§ 24-4-412. Complainant's past sexual behavior not admissible in prosecutions for certain sexual offenses; exceptions

(a) In any prosecution for rape in violation of Code Section 16-6-1; aggravated assault with the intent to rape in violation of Code Section 16-5-21; aggravated sodomy or sodomy in violation of Code Section 16-6-2; statutory rape in violation of Code Section 16-6-3; aggravated child molestation or child molestation in violation of Code Section 16-6-4; incest in violation of Code Section 16-6-22; sexual battery in violation of Code Section 16-6-22.1; or aggravated sexual battery in violation of Code Section 16-6-22.2, evidence relating to the past sexual behavior of the complaining witness shall not be admissible, either as direct evidence or on cross-examination of the complaining witness or other witnesses, except as provided in this Code section. For the purposes of this Code section, evidence of past sexual behavior includes, but is not limited to, evidence of the complaining witness's marital history, mode of dress, general reputation for promiscuity, nonchastity, or sexual mores contrary to the community standards.

(b) In any prosecution for rape in violation of Code Section 16-6-1; aggravated assault with the intent to rape in violation of Code Section 16-5-21; aggravated sodomy or sodomy in violation of Code Section 16-6-2; statutory rape in violation of Code Section 16-6-3; aggravated child molestation or child molestation in violation of Code Section 16-6-4; incest in violation of Code Section 16-6-22; sexual battery in violation of Code Section 16-6-22.1; or aggravated sexual battery in violation of Code Section 16-6-22.2, evidence relating to the past sexual behavior of the complaining witness may be introduced if the court, following the procedure described in subsection (c) of this Code section, finds that the past sexual behavior directly involved the participation of the accused and finds that the evidence expected to be introduced supports an inference that the accused could have reasonably believed that the complaining witness consented to the conduct complained of in the prosecution.

(c) The procedure for introducing evidence as described in subsection (b) of this Code section shall be as follows:

    (1) At the time the defense seeks to introduce evidence which would be covered by subsection (b) of this Code section, the defense shall notify the court of such intent, whereupon the court shall conduct an in camera hearing to examine the accused's offer of proof;

    (2) At the conclusion of the hearing, if the court finds that any of the evidence introduced at the hearing is admissible under subsection (b) of this Code section or is so highly material that it will substantially support a conclusion that the accused reasonably believed that the complaining witness consented to the conduct complained of and that justice mandates the admission of such evidence, the court shall by order state what evidence may be introduced by the defense at the trial of the case and in what manner the evidence may be introduced; and

    (3) The defense may then introduce evidence pursuant to the order of the court.

§ 24-4-413. Evidence of similar transaction crimes in sexual assault cases

(a) In a criminal proceeding in which the accused is accused of an offense of sexual assault, evidence of the accused's commission of another offense of sexual assault shall be admissible and may be considered for its bearing on any matter to which it is relevant.

(b) In a proceeding in which the prosecution intends to offer evidence under this Code section, the prosecutor shall disclose such evidence to the accused, including statements of witnesses or a summary of the substance of any testimony that is expected to be offered, at least ten days in advance of trial, unless the time is shortened or lengthened or pretrial notice is excused by the judge upon good cause shown.

(c) This Code section shall not be the exclusive means to admit or consider evidence described in this Code section.

(d) As used in this Code section, the term "offense of sexual assault" means any conduct or attempt or conspiracy to engage in:

    (1) Conduct that would be a violation of Code Section 16-6-1, 16-6-2, 16-6-3, 16-6-5.1, 16-6-22, 16-6-22.1, or 16-6-22.2;

    (2) Any crime that involves contact, without consent, between any part of the accused's body or an object and the genitals or anus of another person;

    (3) Any crime that involves contact, without consent, between the genitals or anus of the accused and any part of another person's body; or

    (4) Any crime that involves deriving sexual pleasure or gratification from the infliction of death, bodily injury, or physical pain on another person.

§ 24-4-414. Evidence of similar transaction crimes in child molestation cases

(a) In a criminal proceeding in which the accused is accused of an offense of child molestation, evidence of the accused's commission of another offense of child molestation shall be admissible and may be considered for its bearing on any matter to which it is relevant.

(b) In a proceeding in which the state intends to offer evidence under this Code section, the prosecuting attorney shall disclose the evidence to the accused, including statements of witnesses or a summary of the substance of any testimony that the prosecuting attorney expects to offer, at least ten days in advance of trial, unless the time is shortened or lengthened or pretrial notice is excused by the judge upon good cause shown.

(c) This Code section shall not be the exclusive means to admit or consider evidence described under this Code section.

(d) As used in this Code section, the term "offense of child molestation" means any conduct or attempt or conspiracy to engage in:

　(1) Conduct that would be a violation of Code Section 16-6-4, 16-6-5, 16-12-100, 16-12-100.2, or 16-12-100.3;

　(2) Any crime that involves contact between any part of the accused's body or an object and the genitals or anus of a child;

　(3) Any crime that involves contact between the genitals or anus of the accused and any part of the body of a child; or

　(4) Any crime that involves deriving sexual pleasure or gratification from the infliction of death, bodily injury, or physical pain on a child.

§ 24-4-415. Evidence of similar acts in civil or administrative proceedings concerning sexual assault or child molestation

(a) In a civil or administrative proceeding in which a claim for damages or other relief is predicated on a party's alleged commission of conduct constituting an offense of sexual assault or an offense of child molestation, evidence of that party's commission of another offense of sexual assault or another offense of child molestation shall be admissible and may be considered as provided in Code Sections 24-4-413 and 24-4-414.

(b) A party who intends to offer evidence under this Code section shall disclose the evidence to the party against whom it will be offered, including statements of witnesses or a summary of the substance of any testimony that is expected to be offered, at least ten days in advance of trial, unless the time is shortened or lengthened or pretrial notice is excused by the judge upon good cause shown.

(c) This Code section shall not be the exclusive means to admit or consider evidence described in this Code section.

(d) As used in this Code section, the term:

　(1) "Offense of child molestation" means any conduct or attempt or conspiracy to engage in:

(A) Conduct that would be a violation of Code Section 16-6-4, 16-6-5, 16-12-100, 16-12-100.2, or 16-12-100.3;

(B) Any crime that involves contact between any part of the accused's body or an object and the genitals or anus of a child;

(C) Any crime that involves contact between the genitals or anus of the accused and any part of the body of a child; or

(D) Any crime that involves deriving sexual pleasure or gratification from the infliction of death, bodily injury, or physical pain on a child.

(2) "Offense of sexual assault" means any conduct or attempt or conspiracy to engage in:

(A) Conduct that would be a violation of Code Section 16-6-1, 16-6-2, 16-6-3, 16-6-5.1, 16-6-22, 16-6-22.1, or 16-6-22.2;

(B) Any crime that involves contact, without consent, between any part of the accused's body or an object and the genitals or anus of another person;

(C) Any crime that involves contact, without consent, between the genitals or anus of the accused and any part of another person's body; or

(D) Any crime that involves deriving sexual pleasure or gratification from the infliction of death, bodily injury, or physical pain on another person.

§ 24-4-416. Statements of sympathy in medical malpractice cases

(a) As used in this Code section, the term "health care provider" means any person licensed under Chapter 9, 10A, 11, 11A, 26, 28, 30, 33, 34, 35, 39, or 44 of Title 43 or any hospital, nursing home, home health agency, institution, or medical facility licensed or defined under Chapter 7 of Title 31. The term shall also include any corporation, professional corporation, partnership, limited liability company, limited liability partnership, authority, or other entity composed of such health care providers.

(b) In any claim or civil proceeding brought by or on behalf of a patient allegedly experiencing an unanticipated outcome of medical care, any and all statements, affirmations, gestures, activities, or conduct expressing regret, apology, sympathy, commiseration, condolence, compassion, mistake, error, or a general sense of benevolence which is made by a health care provider or an employee or agent of a health care provider to the patient, a relative of the patient, or a representative of the patient and which relates to the unanticipated outcome shall be inadmissible as evidence and shall not constitute an admission of liability or an admission against interest.

§ 24-4-417. Evidence of similar acts in prosecutions for violations of Code Section 40-6-391

(a) In a criminal proceeding involving a prosecution for a violation of Code Section 40-6-391, evidence of the commission of another violation of Code Section 40-6-391 on a different occasion by the same accused shall be admissible when:
   (1) The accused refused in the current case to take the state administered test required by Code Section 40-5-55 and such evidence is relevant to prove knowledge, plan, or absence of mistake or accident;
   (2) The accused refused in the current case to provide an adequate breath sample for the state administered test required by Code Section 40-5-55 and such evidence is relevant to prove knowledge, plan, or absence of mistake or accident; or
   (3) The identity of the driver is in dispute in the current case and such evidence is relevant to prove identity.
(b) In a criminal proceeding in which the state intends to offer evidence under this Code section, the prosecuting attorney shall disclose such evidence to the accused, including statements of witnesses or a summary of the substance of any testimony that the prosecuting attorney expects to offer, at least ten days in advance of trial, unless the time is shortened or pretrial notice is excused by the judge upon good cause shown.
(c) This Code section shall not be the exclusive means to admit or consider evidence described in this Code section.

§ 24-4-418. Admissibility of criminal gang activity, disclosure

(a) In a criminal proceeding in which the accused is accused of conducting or participating in criminal gang activity in violation of Code Section 16-15-4, evidence of the accused's commission of criminal gang activity, as such term is defined in Code Section 16-15-3, shall be admissible and may be considered for its bearing on any matter to which it is relevant.
(b) In a proceeding in which the prosecution intends to offer evidence under this Code section, the prosecutor shall disclose such evidence to the accused, including statements of witnesses or a summary of the substance of any testimony that is expected to be offered, at least ten days in advance of trial, unless the time is shortened or lengthened or pretrial notice is excused by the judge upon good cause shown.
(c) This Code section shall not be the exclusive means to admit or consider evidence described in this Code section.

CHAPTER 5. PRIVILEGES

§ 24-5-501. Certain communications privileged

(a) There are certain admissions and communications excluded from evidence on grounds of public policy, including, but not limited to, the following:

(1) Communications between husband and wife;

(2) Communications between attorney and client;

(3) Communications among grand jurors;

(4) Secrets of state;

(5) Communications between psychiatrist and patient;

(6) Communications between licensed psychologist and patient as provided in Code Section 43-39-16;

(7) Communications between a licensed clinical social worker, clinical nurse specialist in psychiatric/mental health, licensed marriage and family therapist, or licensed professional counselor and patient;

(8) Communications between or among any psychiatrist, psychologist, licensed clinical social worker, clinical nurse specialist in psychiatric/mental health, licensed marriage and family therapist, and licensed professional counselor who are rendering psychotherapy or have rendered psychotherapy to a patient, regarding that patient's communications which are otherwise privileged by paragraph (5), (6), or (7) of this subsection; and

(9) Communications between accountant and client as provided by Code Section 43-3-29.

(b) As used in this Code section, the term:

(1) "Psychotherapy" means the employment of psychotherapeutic techniques.

(2) "Psychotherapeutic techniques" shall have the same meaning as provided in Code Section 43-10A-3.

§ 24-5-502. Communications to clergyman privileged

Every communication made by any person professing religious faith, seeking spiritual comfort, or seeking counseling to any Protestant minister of the Gospel, any priest of the Roman Catholic faith, any priest of the Greek Orthodox Catholic faith, any Jewish rabbi, or any Christian or Jewish minister or similar functionary, by whatever name called, shall be deemed privileged. No such minister, priest, rabbi, or similar functionary shall disclose any communications made to him or her by any such person professing religious faith, seeking spiritual guidance, or seeking counseling, nor shall such minister, priest, rabbi, or similar functionary be competent or compellable to testify with reference to any such communication in any court.

§ 24-5-503. Husband and wife as witnesses for and against each other in criminal proceedings

(a) A husband and wife shall be competent but shall not be compellable to give evidence in any criminal proceeding for or against each other.

(b) The privilege created by subsection (a) of this Code section or by corresponding privileges in paragraph (1) of subsection (a) of Code Section 24-5-501 or subsection (a) of Code Section 24-5-505 shall not apply in proceedings in which:

(1) The husband or wife is charged with a crime against the person of a child under the age of 18, but such husband or wife shall be compellable to give evidence only on the specific act for which the accused is charged;

(2) The husband or wife is charged with a crime against his or her spouse;

(3) The husband or wife is charged with causing physical damage to property belonging to the husband and wife or to their separate property; or

(4) The alleged crime against his or her current spouse occurred prior to the lawful marriage of the husband and wife.

§ 24-5-504. Law enforcement officers testifying; home address

Any law enforcement officer testifying in his or her official capacity in any criminal proceeding shall not be compelled to reveal his or her home address. Such officer may be required to divulge the business address of his or her employer, and the court may require any law enforcement officer to answer questions as to his or her home address whenever such fact may be material to any issue in the proceeding.

§ 24-5-505. Party or witness privilege

(a) No party or witness shall be required to testify as to any matter which may incriminate or tend to incriminate such party or witness or which shall tend to bring infamy, disgrace, or public contempt upon such party or witness or any member of such party or witness's family.

(b) Except in proceedings in which a judgment creditor or judgment creditor's successor in interest seeks postjudgment discovery involving a judgment debtor pursuant to Code Section 9-11-69, no party or witness shall be required to testify as to any matter which shall tend to work a forfeiture of his or her estate.

(c) No official persons shall be called on to disclose any state matters of which the policy of the state and the interest of the community require concealment.

§ 24-5-506. Privilege against self-incrimination; testimony of accused in criminal case

(a) No person who is charged in any criminal proceeding with the commission of any criminal offense shall be compellable to give evidence for or against himself or herself.

(b) If an accused in a criminal proceeding wishes to testify and announces in open court his or her intention to do so, the accused may so testify. If an accused testifies, he or she shall be sworn as any other witness and, except as provided in Code Sections 24-6-608 and 24-6-609, may be examined and cross-examined as any other witness. The failure of an accused to testify shall create no presumption against the accused, and no comment shall be made because of such failure.

§ 24-5-507. Grant of immunity; contempt

(a) Whenever in the judgment of the Attorney General or any district attorney the testimony of any person or the production of evidence of any kind by any person in any criminal proceeding before a court or grand jury is necessary to the public interest, the Attorney General or the district attorney may request in writing the superior court to order such person to testify or produce the evidence. Upon order of the court, such person shall not be excused on the basis of the privilege against self-incrimination from testifying or producing any evidence required, but no testimony or other evidence required under the order or any information directly or indirectly derived from such testimony or evidence shall be used against the person in any proceeding or prosecution for a crime or offense concerning which he or she testified or produced evidence under court order. However, such person may nevertheless be prosecuted or subjected to penalty or forfeiture for any perjury, false swearing, or contempt committed in testifying or failing to testify or in producing or failing to produce evidence in accordance with the order but shall not be required to produce evidence that can be used in any other court of this state, the United States, or any other state. Any order entered under this Code section shall be entered of record in the minutes of the court so as to afford a permanent record thereof, and any testimony given by a person pursuant to such order shall be transcribed and filed for permanent record in the office of the clerk of the court.

(b) If a person refuses to testify after being granted immunity from prosecution and after being ordered to testify as set forth in this Code section, such person may be adjudged in contempt and committed to the county jail until such time as such person purges himself or herself of contempt by testifying as ordered without regard to the expiration of the grand jury. If the grand jury before which such person was ordered to testify has been dissolved, such person may purge himself or herself by testifying before the court.

§ 24-5-508. Qualified privilege for news gathering or dissemination

Any person, company, or other entity engaged in the gathering and dissemination of news for the public through any newspaper, book, magazine, radio or television broadcast, or electronic means shall have a qualified privilege against disclosure of any information, document, or item obtained or prepared in the gathering or dissemination of news in any proceeding where the one asserting the privilege is not a party, unless it is shown that this privilege has been waived or that what is sought:

(1) Is material and relevant;

(2) Cannot be reasonably obtained by alternative means; and

(3) Is necessary to the proper preparation or presentation of the case of a party seeking the information, document, or item.

§ 24-5-509. Communications between victim of family violence or sexual assault and agents providing services to such victim; termination of privilege

(a) As used in this Code section, the term:
  (1) "Agent" means a current or former employee or volunteer of a program who has successfully completed a minimum of 20 hours of training in family violence and sexual assault intervention and prevention at a Criminal Justice Coordinating Council certified victim assistance program.
  (2) "Family violence" shall have the same meaning as provided in Code Section 19-13-1.
  (3) "Family violence shelter" means a program whose primary purpose is to provide services to family violence victims and their families that is not under the direct supervision of a law enforcement agency, prosecuting attorney's office, or a government agency.
  (4) "Family violence victim" means a person who consults a family violence shelter for the purpose of securing advice or other services concerning an act of family violence, an alleged act of family violence, or an attempted act of family violence.
  (5) "Government agency" means any agency of the executive, legislative, or judicial branch of government or political subdivision or authority thereof of this state, any other state, the District of Columbia, the United States and its territories and possessions, or any foreign government or international governmental or quasi-governmental agency recognized by the United States or by any of the several states.
  (6) "Negative effect of the disclosure of the evidence on the victim" shall include the impact of the disclosure on the relationship between the victim and the agent and the delivery and accessibility of services.
  (7) "Program" means a family violence shelter or rape crisis center.
  (8) "Rape crisis center" means a program whose primary purpose is to provide services to sexual assault victims and their families that is not under the direct supervision of a law enforcement agency, prosecuting attorney's office, or a government agency.
  (9) "Services" means any services provided to a victim by a program including but not limited to crisis hot lines, safe homes and shelters, assessment and intake, counseling, services for children who are victims of family violence or sexual assault, support in medical, administrative, and judicial systems, transportation, relocation, and crisis intervention. Such term shall not include mandatory reporting as required by Code Section 19-7-5 or 30-5-4.

(10) "Sexual assault" shall have the same meaning as provided in Code Section 17-5-70.

(11) "Sexual assault victim" means a person who consults a rape crisis center for the purpose of securing advice or other services concerning a sexual assault, an alleged sexual assault, or an attempted sexual assault.

(12) "Victim" means a family violence victim or sexual assault victim.

(b) No agent of a program shall be compelled to disclose any evidence in a judicial proceeding that the agent acquired while providing services to a victim, provided that such evidence was necessary to enable the agent to render services, unless the privilege has been waived by the victim or, upon motion by a party, the court finds by a preponderance of the evidence at a pretrial hearing or hearing outside the presence of the jury that:

(1) In a civil proceeding:

(A) The evidence sought is material and relevant to factual issues to be determined;

(B) The evidence is not sought solely for the purpose of referring to the victim's character for truthfulness or untruthfulness; provided, however, that this subparagraph shall not apply to evidence of the victim's prior inconsistent statements;

(C) The evidence sought is not available or already obtained by the party seeking disclosure; and

(D) The probative value of the evidence sought substantially outweighs the negative effect of the disclosure of the evidence on the victim; or

(2) In a criminal proceeding:

(A) The evidence sought is material and relevant to the issue of guilt, degree of guilt, or sentencing for the offense charged or a lesser included offense;

(B) The evidence is not sought solely for the purpose of referring to the victim's character for truthfulness or untruthfulness; provided, however, that this subparagraph shall not apply to evidence of the victim's prior inconsistent statements;

(C) The evidence sought is not available or already obtained by the party seeking disclosure; and

(D) The probative value of the evidence sought substantially outweighs the negative effect of the disclosure of the evidence on the victim.

(c) If the court finds that the evidence sought may be subject to disclosure pursuant to subsection (b) of this Code section, the court shall order that such evidence be produced for the court under seal, shall examine the evidence in camera, and may allow disclosure of those portions of the evidence that the court finds are subject to disclosure under this Code section.

(d) The privilege afforded under this Code section shall terminate upon the death of the victim.

(e) The privilege granted by this Code section shall not apply if the agent was a witness or party to the family violence or sexual assault or other crime that occurred in the agent's presence.

(f) The mere presence of a third person during communications between an agent and a victim shall not void the privilege granted by this Code section, provided that the communication occurred in a setting when or where the victim had a reasonable expectation of privacy.

(g) If the victim is or has been judicially determined to be incompetent, the victim's guardian may waive the victim's privilege.

(h) In criminal proceedings, if either party intends to compel evidence based on this Code section, the party shall file and serve notice of his or her intention on the opposing party at least ten days prior to trial, or as otherwise directed by the court. The court shall hold a pretrial hearing in accordance with subsection (b) of this Code section and determine the issue prior to trial.

§ 24-5-510. (For effective date, see note.) Privileged communications between law enforcement officers and peer counselors

(a) As used in this Code section, the term:
  (1) "Client" means a law enforcement employee or a law enforcement officer's immediate family.
  (2) "Immediate family" means the spouse, child, stepchild, parent, or stepparent.
  (3) "Peer counselor" means an employee of a law enforcement agency who has received training to provide emotional and moral support to a client and was designated by a sheriff, police chief, or other head of a law enforcement agency to counsel clients.

(b) Except as provided in subsection (c) of this Code section, communications between a client and a peer counselor shall be privileged. A peer counselor shall not disclose any such communications made to him or her and shall not be competent or compellable to testify with reference to any such communications in any court.

(c) The privilege created by subsection (b) of this Code section shall not apply when:
  (1) The disclosure is authorized by the client, or if the client is deceased, by his or her executor or administrator, and if an executor or administrator is not appointed, by the client's next of kin;
  (2) Compelled by court order;
  (3) The peer counselor was an initial responding officer, witness, or party to an act that is the subject of the counseling;
  (4) The communication was made when the peer counselor was not performing official duties; or
  (5) The client is charged with a crime.

(d) The privilege created by this Code section shall not be grounds to fail to comply with mandatory reporting requirements as set forth in Code Section 19-7-5 or Chapter 5 of Title 30, the "Disabled Adults and Elder Persons Protection Act."

CHAPTER 6. WITNESSES

ARTICLE 1. GENERAL PROVISIONS

§ 24-6-601. General rule of competency

Except as otherwise provided in this chapter, every person is competent to be a witness.

§ 24-6-602. Lack of personal knowledge

A witness may not testify to a matter unless evidence is introduced sufficient to support a finding that the witness has personal knowledge of such matter. Evidence to prove personal knowledge may, but need not, consist of the witness's own testimony. The provisions of this Code section are subject to Code Section 24-7-703 and shall not apply to party admissions.

§ 24-6-603. Oath or affirmation

(a) Before testifying, every witness shall be required to declare that he or she will testify truthfully by oath or affirmation administered in a form calculated to awaken the witness's conscience and impress the witness's mind with the duty to do so.

(b) Notwithstanding the provisions of subsection (a) of this Code section, in all proceedings involving dependency as defined by Code Section 15-11-2 and in all criminal proceedings in which a child was a victim of or witness to any crime, the child shall be competent to testify, and the child's credibility shall be determined as provided in this chapter.

§ 24-6-604. Interpreters

Except as provided in Code Sections 24-6-656 and 24-6-657 or by the rules promulgated by the Supreme Court of Georgia pursuant to Code Section 15-1-14, an interpreter shall be subject to the provisions of Code Section 24-7-702. Interpreters shall be required to take an oath or affirmation to make a true translation.

§ 24-6-605. Judge as witness

The judge presiding at the trial shall not testify in that trial as a witness. No objection need be made in order to preserve this issue.

§ 24-6-606. Juror as witness

(a) A member of the jury shall not testify as a witness before that jury in the trial of the case in which the juror is sitting. If a juror is called to testify, the opposing party shall be afforded an opportunity to object out of the presence of the jury.

(b) Upon an inquiry into the validity of a verdict or indictment, a juror shall not testify by affidavit or otherwise nor shall a juror's statements be received in evidence as to any matter or statement occurring during the course of the jury's deliberations or to the effect of anything upon the jury deliberations or any other juror's mind or emotions as influencing the juror to assent to or dissent from the verdict or indictment or concerning the juror's mental processes in connection therewith; provided, however, that a juror may testify on the question of whether extraneous prejudicial information was improperly brought to the juror's attention, whether any outside influence was improperly brought to bear upon any juror, or whether there was a mistake in entering the verdict onto the verdict form.

§ 24-6-607. Who may impeach

The credibility of a witness may be attacked by any party, including the party calling the witness.

§ 24-6-608. Evidence of character and conduct of witness

(a) The credibility of a witness may be attacked or supported by evidence in the form of opinion or reputation, subject to the following limitations:
   (1) The evidence may refer only to character for truthfulness or untruthfulness; and
   (2) Evidence of truthful character shall be admissible only after the character of the witness for truthfulness has been attacked by opinion or reputation evidence or otherwise.

(b) Specific instances of the conduct of a witness, for the purpose of attacking or supporting the witness's character for truthfulness, other than a conviction of a crime as provided in Code Section 24-6-609, or conduct indicative of the witness's bias toward a party may not be proved by extrinsic evidence. Such instances may however, in the discretion of the court, if probative of truthfulness or untruthfulness, be inquired into on cross-examination of the witness:
   (1) Concerning the witness's character for truthfulness or untruthfulness; or
   (2) Concerning the character for truthfulness or untruthfulness of another witness as to which character the witness being cross-examined has testified.

(c) The giving of testimony, whether by an accused or by any other witness, shall not operate as a waiver of the accused's or the witness's privilege against self-incrimination when examined with respect to matters which relate only to character for truthfulness.

§ 24-6-609. Impeachment by evidence of conviction of a crime

(a) General rule. For the purpose of attacking the character for truthfulness of a witness:

    (1) Evidence that a witness other than an accused has been convicted of a crime shall be admitted subject to the provisions of Code Section 24-4-403 if the crime was punishable by death or imprisonment in excess of one year under the law under which the witness was convicted and evidence that an accused has been convicted of such a crime shall be admitted if the court determines that the probative value of admitting the evidence outweighs its prejudicial effect to the accused; or

    (2) Evidence that any witness has been convicted of a crime shall be admitted regardless of the punishment, if it readily can be determined that establishing the elements of such crime required proof or admission of an act of dishonesty or making a false statement.

(b) Time limit. Evidence of a conviction under this Code section shall not be admissible if a period of more than ten years has elapsed since the date of the conviction or of the release of the witness from the confinement imposed for such conviction, whichever is the later date, unless the court determines, in the interests of justice, that the probative value of the conviction supported by specific facts and circumstances substantially outweighs its prejudicial effect. However, evidence of a conviction more than ten years old, as calculated in this subsection, shall not be admissible unless the proponent gives to the adverse party sufficient advance written notice of intent to use such evidence to provide the adverse party with a fair opportunity to contest the use of such evidence.

(c) Effect of pardon, annulment, certificate of rehabilitation, or discharge from a first offender program. Evidence of a final adjudication of guilt and subsequent discharge under any first offender statute shall not be used to impeach any witness and evidence of a conviction shall not be admissible under this Code section if:

    (1) The conviction has been the subject of a pardon, annulment, certificate of rehabilitation, or other equivalent procedure based on a finding of the rehabilitation of the person convicted, and that person has not been convicted of a subsequent crime which was punishable by death or imprisonment in excess of one year; or

    (2) The conviction has been the subject of a pardon, annulment, or other equivalent procedure based on a finding of innocence.

(d) Nolo contendere pleas and juvenile adjudications. A conviction based on a plea of nolo contendere shall not be admissible to impeach any witness under this Code section. Evidence of juvenile adjudications shall not generally be admissible under this Code section. The court may, however, in a criminal proceeding allow evidence of a juvenile adjudication of a witness other than the accused if conviction of the offense would be admissible to attack the credibility of an adult and the court is satisfied that admission in evidence is necessary for a fair determination of the issue of guilt or innocence of the accused.

(e) Pendency of appeal. The pendency of an appeal shall not render evidence of a conviction inadmissible. Evidence of the pendency of an appeal shall be admissible.

§ 24-6-610. Religious beliefs or opinions

Evidence of the beliefs or opinions of a witness on matters of religion shall not be admissible for the purpose of proving that by reason of the nature of the beliefs or opinions the witness's credibility is impaired or enhanced.

§ 24-6-611. Mode and order of witness interrogation and presentation

(a) The court shall exercise reasonable control over the mode and order of interrogating witnesses and presenting evidence so as to:
   (1) Make the interrogation and presentation effective for the ascertainment of the truth;
   (2) Avoid needless consumption of time; and
   (3) Protect witnesses from harassment or undue embarrassment.
(b) A witness may be cross-examined on any matter relevant to any issue in the proceeding. The right of a thorough and sifting cross-examination shall belong to every party as to the witnesses called against the party. If several parties to the same proceeding have distinct interests, each party may exercise the right to cross-examination.
(c) Leading questions shall not be used on the direct examination of a witness except as may be necessary to develop the witness's testimony. Ordinarily leading questions shall be permitted on cross-examination. When a party calls a hostile witness, an adverse party, or a witness identified with an adverse party, interrogation may be by leading questions.

§ 24-6-612. Writing used to refresh memory

(a) If a witness uses a writing to refresh his or her memory while testifying, an adverse party shall be entitled to have the writing produced at the hearing or trial, to inspect it, to cross-examine the witness on such writing, and to introduce in evidence those portions of such writing which relate to the testimony of the witness.
(b) If a witness uses a writing to refresh his or her memory before testifying at trial and the court in its discretion determines it is necessary in the interests of justice, an adverse party shall be entitled to have the writing produced at the trial, to inspect it, to cross-examine the witness on such writing, and to introduce in evidence those portions of such writing which relate to the testimony of the witness. If the writing used is protected by the attorney-client privilege or as attorney work product under Code

Section 9-11-26, use of the writing to refresh recollection prior to testifying shall not constitute a waiver of that privilege or protection. If it is claimed that the writing contains matters not related to the subject matter of the testimony, the court shall examine the writing in camera, excise any portions of such writing not so related, and order delivery of the remainder of such writing to the party entitled to such writing. Any portion withheld over objections shall be preserved and made available to the appellate court in the event of an appeal. If a writing is not produced or delivered pursuant to an order under this Code section, the court shall make any order justice requires; provided, however, that in criminal proceedings, when the prosecution elects not to comply, the order shall be one striking the testimony or, if the court in its discretion determines that the interests of justice so require, declaring a mistrial.

§ 24-6-613. Prior statements of witnesses

(a) In examining a witness concerning a prior statement made by the witness, whether written or not, the statement need not be shown nor its contents disclosed to the witness at that time; provided, however, upon request the same shall be shown or disclosed to opposing counsel.

(b) Except as provided in Code Section 24-8-806, extrinsic evidence of a prior inconsistent statement by a witness shall not be admissible unless the witness is first afforded an opportunity to explain or deny the prior inconsistent statement and the opposite party is afforded an opportunity to interrogate the witness on the prior inconsistent statement or the interests of justice otherwise require. This subsection shall not apply to admissions of a party-opponent as set forth in paragraph (2) of subsection (d) of Code Section 24-8-801.

(c) A prior consistent statement shall be admissible to rehabilitate a witness if the prior consistent statement logically rebuts an attack made on the witness's credibility. A general attack on a witness's credibility with evidence offered under Code Section 24-6-608 or 24-6-609 shall not permit rehabilitation under this subsection. If a prior consistent statement is offered to rebut an express or implied charge against the witness of recent fabrication or improper influence or motive, the prior consistent statement shall have been made before the alleged recent fabrication or improper influence or motive arose.

§ 24-6-614. Calling and interrogation of witnesses by court

(a) The court may, on its own motion, call a court appointed expert, call a witness regarding the competency of any party, or call a child witness or, at the suggestion of a party, call such witnesses, and all parties shall be entitled to cross-examine such witnesses. In all other situations, the court may only call witnesses when there is an agreement of all of the parties for the court to call such witnesses and all parties shall be entitled to cross-examine such witnesses.

(b) The court may interrogate witnesses whether called by itself pursuant to subsection (a) of this Code section or by a party.

(c) Objections to the calling of witnesses by the court or to interrogation by the court may be made at the time or at the next available opportunity when the jury is not present.

§ 24-6-615. Exclusion of witnesses

Except as otherwise provided in Code Section 24-6-616, at the request of a party the court shall order witnesses excluded so that each witness cannot hear the testimony of other witnesses, and it may make the order on its own motion. This Code section shall not authorize exclusion of:

(1) A party who is a natural person;

(2) An officer or employee of a party which is not a natural person designated as its representative by its attorney; or

(3) A person whose presence is shown by a party to be essential to the presentation of the party's cause.

§ 24-6-616. Presence in courtroom of victim of criminal offense

Subject to the provisions of Code Section 17-17-9, the victim of a criminal offense shall be entitled to be present in any court exercising jurisdiction over such offense.

ARTICLE 2. CREDIBILITY

§ 24-6-620. Credibility a jury question

The credibility of a witness shall be a matter to be determined by the trier of fact, and if the case is being heard by a jury, the court shall give the jury proper instructions as to the credibility of a witness.

§ 24-6-621. Impeachment by contradiction

A witness may be impeached by disproving the facts testified to by the witness.

§ 24-6-622. Witness's feelings and relationship to parties provable

The state of a witness's feelings towards the parties and the witness's relationship to the parties may always be proved for the consideration of the jury.

§ 24-6-623. Treatment of witness

It shall be the right of a witness to be examined only as to relevant matters and to be protected from improper questions and from harsh or insulting demeanor.

ARTICLE 3. USE OF SIGN LANGUAGE AND INTERMEDIARY INTERPRETER IN ADMINISTRATIVE AND JUDICIAL PROCEEDINGS

§ 24-6-650. State policy on hearing impaired persons

It is the policy of the State of Georgia to secure the rights of hearing impaired persons who, because of impaired hearing, cannot readily understand or communicate in spoken language and who consequently cannot equally participate in or benefit from proceedings, programs, and activities of the courts, legislative bodies, administrative agencies, licensing commissions, departments, and boards of this state and its political subdivisions unless qualified interpreters are available to assist such persons.

§ 24-6-651. Definitions

As used in this article, the term:
  (1) "Agency" means any agency, authority, board, bureau, committee, commission, court, department, or jury of the legislative, judicial, or executive branch of government of this state or any political subdivision thereof.
  (2) "Court qualified interpreter" means any person licensed as an interpreter for the hearing impaired pursuant to Code Section 15-1-14.
  (3) "Hearing impaired person" means any person whose hearing is totally impaired or whose hearing is so seriously impaired as to prohibit the person from understanding oral communications when spoken in a normal conversational tone.
  (4) "Intermediary interpreter" means any person, including any hearing impaired person, who is able to assist in providing an accurate interpretation between spoken English and sign language or between the variance of sign language by acting as an intermediary between a hearing impaired person and a qualified interpreter.
  (5) "Proceeding" means any meeting, hearing, trial, investigation, or other proceeding of any nature conducted by an agency.
  (6) "Qualified interpreter" means any person certified as an interpreter for hearing impaired persons by the Registry of Interpreters for the Deaf or a court qualified interpreter.

§ 24-6-652. Appointment of interpreters for hearing impaired persons interested in or witness at agency proceedings

(a) The agency conducting any proceeding shall provide a qualified interpreter to the hearing impaired person:
  (1) Whenever the hearing impaired person is a party to the proceeding or a witness before the proceeding; or

(2) Whenever a person who is below the age of 18 years is a party to the proceeding or a witness before the proceeding conducted by an agency whose parents are hearing impaired persons or whose guardian is a hearing impaired person.

(b) A hearing impaired person shall notify the agency not less than ten days, excluding weekends and holidays, prior to the date of the proceeding of the need for a qualified interpreter. If the hearing impaired person received notice of the proceeding less than ten days, excluding weekends and holidays, prior to the proceeding, such person shall notify the agency as soon as practicable after receiving such notice.

§ 24-6-653. Procedure for interrogation and taking of statements from hearing impaired persons arrested for violation of criminal laws

(a) An arresting law enforcement agency shall provide a qualified interpreter to any hearing impaired person whenever a hearing impaired person is arrested for allegedly violating any criminal law or ordinance of this state or any political subdivision thereof.

(b)

(1) Except as provided in paragraph (2) of this subsection, no interrogation, warning, informing of rights, taking of statements, or other investigatory procedures shall be undertaken upon a hearing impaired person unless a qualified interpreter has been provided or the law enforcement agency has taken such other steps as may be reasonable to accommodate such person's disability. No answer, statement, admission, or other evidence acquired through the interrogation of a hearing impaired person shall be admissible in any criminal or quasi-criminal proceedings unless such was knowingly and voluntarily given. No hearing impaired person who has been taken into custody and who is otherwise eligible for release shall be detained because of the unavailability of a qualified interpreter.

(2) If a qualified interpreter is not available, an arresting officer may interrogate or take a statement from such person, provided that if the hearing impaired person cannot hear spoken words with a hearing aid or other sound amplification device, such interrogation and answers thereto shall be in writing and shall be preserved and turned over to the court in the event such person is tried for the alleged offense.

§ 24-6-654. Indigent hearing impaired defendants to be provided with interpreters

(a) A court shall provide a court qualified interpreter to any hearing impaired person whenever the hearing impaired person has been provided with a public defender or court appointed legal counsel.

(b) The court qualified interpreter authorized by this Code section shall be present at all times when the hearing impaired person is consulting with legal counsel.

§ 24-6-655. Waiver of right to interpreter

Whenever a hearing impaired person shall be authorized to be provided a qualified interpreter, such person may waive the right to the use of such interpreter. Any such waiver shall be in writing and shall be approved by the agency or law enforcement agency before which the hearing impaired person is to appear. In no event shall the failure of a hearing impaired person to request an interpreter be deemed to be a waiver of the hearing impaired person's right to a qualified interpreter.

§ 24-6-656. Replacement of interpreters unable to communicate accurately with hearing impaired persons; appointment of intermediary interpreters

Whenever a hearing impaired person shall be authorized to be provided a qualified interpreter, the agency or law enforcement agency shall determine whether the qualified interpreter so provided is able to communicate accurately with and translate information to and from the hearing impaired person. If it is determined that the qualified interpreter cannot perform these functions, the agency or law enforcement agency shall obtain the services of another qualified interpreter or shall appoint an intermediary interpreter to assist the qualified interpreter in communicating with the hearing impaired person.

§ 24-6-657. Oath of interpreters; privileged communications; taping and filming of hearing impaired persons' testimony

(a) Prior to providing any service to a hearing impaired person, any qualified interpreter or intermediary interpreter shall subscribe to an oath that he or she will interpret all communications in an accurate manner to the best of his or her skill and knowledge. The Supreme Court of Georgia may by rule of court prescribe the form of the oath for interpreters and intermediary interpreters for use in court and other judicial proceedings.

(b) Whenever a hearing impaired person communicates with any other person through the use of an interpreter and under circumstances which make such communications privileged or otherwise confidential, the presence of the interpreter shall not vitiate such privilege and the interpreter shall not be required to disclose the contents of such communication.

(c) Whenever a qualified interpreter is required by this article, the agency or law enforcement agency shall not begin the proceeding or take any action until such interpreter is in full view of and spatially situated so as to assure effective communication with the hearing impaired person.

(d) The agency or law enforcement agency may, upon its own motion or upon motion of any party, witness, or participant, order that the testimony of the hearing impaired person be electronically and visually recorded. Any such recording may be used to verify the testimony given by the hearing impaired person.

§ 24-6-658. Compensation of interpreters

Any qualified interpreter or intermediary interpreter providing service under this article shall be compensated by the agency or law enforcement agency requesting such service.

CHAPTER 7. OPINIONS AND EXPERT TESTIMONY

§ 24-7-701. Lay witness opinion testimony

(a) If the witness is not testifying as an expert, the witness's testimony in the form of opinions or inferences shall be limited to those opinions or inferences which are:
    (1) Rationally based on the perception of the witness;
    (2) Helpful to a clear understanding of the witness's testimony or the determination of a fact in issue; and
    (3) Not based on scientific, technical, or other specialized knowledge within the scope of Code Section 24-7-702.

(b) Direct testimony as to market value is in the nature of opinion evidence. A witness need not be an expert or dealer in an article or property to testify as to its value if he or she has had an opportunity to form a reasoned opinion.

§ 24-7-702. Expert opinion testimony in civil actions; medical experts; pretrial hearings; precedential value of federal law

(a) Except as provided in Code Section 22-1-14 and in subsection (g) of this Code section, the provisions of this Code section shall apply in all civil proceedings. The opinion of a witness qualified as an expert under this Code section may be given on the facts as proved by other witnesses.

(b) If scientific, technical, or other specialized knowledge will assist the trier of fact to understand the evidence or to determine a fact in issue, a witness qualified as an expert by knowledge, skill, experience, training, or education may testify thereto in the form of an opinion or otherwise, if:
    (1) The testimony is based upon sufficient facts or data;
    (2) The testimony is the product of reliable principles and methods; and
    (3) The witness has applied the principles and methods reliably to the facts of the case which have been or will be admitted into evidence before the trier of fact.

(c) Notwithstanding the provisions of subsection (b) of this Code section and any other provision of law which might be construed to the contrary, in professional malpractice actions, the opinions of an expert, who is otherwise qualified as to the acceptable standard of conduct of the professional whose conduct is at issue, shall be admissible only if, at the time the act or omission is alleged to have occurred, such expert:

(1) Was licensed by an appropriate regulatory agency to practice his or her profession in the state in which such expert was practicing or teaching in the profession at such time; and

(2) In the case of a medical malpractice action, had actual professional knowledge and experience in the area of practice or specialty in which the opinion is to be given as the result of having been regularly engaged in:

(A) The active practice of such area of specialty of his or her profession for at least three of the last five years, with sufficient frequency to establish an appropriate level of knowledge, as determined by the judge, in performing the procedure, diagnosing the condition, or rendering the treatment which is alleged to have been performed or rendered negligently by the defendant whose conduct is at issue; or

(B) The teaching of his or her profession for at least three of the last five years as an employed member of the faculty of an educational institution accredited in the teaching of such profession, with sufficient frequency to establish an appropriate level of knowledge, as determined by the judge, in teaching others how to perform the procedure, diagnose the condition, or render the treatment which is alleged to have been performed or rendered negligently by the defendant whose conduct is at issue; and

(C) Except as provided in subparagraph (D) of this paragraph:

   (i) Is a member of the same profession;

   (ii) Is a medical doctor testifying as to the standard of care of a defendant who is a doctor of osteopathy; or

   (iii) Is a doctor of osteopathy testifying as to the standard of care of a defendant who is a medical doctor; and

(D) Notwithstanding any other provision of this Code section, an expert who is a physician and, as a result of having, during at least three of the last five years immediately preceding the time the act or omission is alleged to have occurred, supervised, taught, or instructed nurses, nurse practitioners, certified registered nurse anesthetists, nurse midwives, physician assistants, physical therapists, occupational therapists, or medical support staff, has knowledge of the standard of care of that health care provider under the circumstances at issue shall be competent to testify as to the standard of that health care provider. However, a nurse, nurse practitioner, certified registered nurse anesthetist, nurse midwife, physician assistant, physical therapist, occupational therapist, or medical support staff shall not be competent to testify as to the standard of care of a physician.

(d) Upon motion of a party, the court may hold a pretrial hearing to determine whether the witness qualifies as an expert and whether the expert's testimony satisfies the requirements of subsections (a) and (b) of this

Code section. Such hearing and ruling shall be completed no later than the final pretrial conference contemplated under Code Section 9-11-16.

(e) An affiant shall meet the requirements of this Code section in order to be deemed qualified to testify as an expert by means of the affidavit required under Code Section 9-11-9.1.

(f) It is the intent of the legislature that, in all civil proceedings, the courts of the State of Georgia not be viewed as open to expert evidence that would not be admissible in other states. Therefore, in interpreting and applying this Code section, the courts of this state may draw from the opinions of the United States Supreme Court in Daubert v. Merrell Dow Pharmaceuticals, Inc., 509 U.S. 579 (1993); General Electric Co. v. Joiner, 522 U.S. 136 (1997); Kumho Tire Co. Ltd. v. Carmichael, 526 U.S. 137 (1999); and other cases in federal courts applying the standards announced by the United States Supreme Court in these cases.

(g) This Code section shall not be strictly applied in proceedings conducted pursuant to Chapter 9 of Title 34 or in administrative proceedings conducted pursuant to Chapter 13 of Title 50.

§ 24-7-703. Bases of expert opinion testimony

The facts or data in the particular proceeding upon which an expert bases an opinion or inference may be those perceived by or made known to the expert at or before the hearing. If of a type reasonably relied upon by experts in the particular field in forming opinions or inferences upon the subject, such facts or data need not be admissible in evidence in order for the opinion or inference to be admitted. Such facts or data that are otherwise inadmissible shall not be disclosed to the jury by the proponent of the opinion or inference unless the court determines that their probative value in assisting the jury to evaluate the expert's opinion substantially outweighs their prejudicial effect.

§ 24-7-704. Ultimate issue opinion

(a) Except as provided in subsection (b) of this Code section, testimony in the form of an opinion or inference otherwise admissible shall not be objectionable because it embraces an ultimate issue to be decided by the trier of fact.

(b) No expert witness testifying with respect to the mental state or condition of an accused in a criminal proceeding shall state an opinion or inference as to whether the accused did or did not have the mental state or condition constituting an element of the crime charged or of a defense thereto. Such ultimate issues are matters for the trier of fact alone.

§ 24-7-705. Disclosure of facts or data underlying expert opinion

An expert may testify in terms of opinion or inference and give reasons therefor without first testifying to the underlying facts or data, unless the court requires otherwise. An expert may in any event be required to disclose the underlying facts or data on cross-examination.

§ 24-7-706. Court appointed experts

Except as provided in Chapter 7 of Title 9 or Code Section 17-7-130.1, 17-10-66, 29-4-11, 29-5-11, 31-14-3, 31-20-3, 44-6-166.1, 44-6-184, or 44-6-187, the following procedures shall govern the appointment, compensation, and presentation of testimony of court appointed experts:

(1) The court on its own motion or on the motion of any party may enter an order to show cause why any expert witness should not be appointed and may request the parties to submit nominations. The court may appoint any expert witnesses agreed upon by the parties and may appoint expert witnesses of its own selection. An expert witness shall not be appointed by the court unless the witness consents to act. Each appointed expert witness shall be informed of his or her duties by the court in writing, a copy of which shall be filed with the clerk, or at a conference in which the parties shall have opportunity to participate. Each appointed expert witness shall advise the parties of his or her findings, if any. Except as provided in Article 3 of Chapter 12 or Article 6 of Chapter 13 of this title, such witness's deposition may be taken by any party. Such witness may be called to testify by the court or any party. Each expert witness shall be subject to cross-examination by each party, including a party calling the witness;

(2) Appointed expert witnesses shall be entitled to reasonable compensation in whatever sum the court allows. The compensation fixed shall be payable from funds which may be provided by law in criminal proceedings and civil proceedings involving just compensation for the taking of property. In other civil proceedings, the compensation shall be paid by the parties in such proportion and at such time as the court directs and thereafter charged in like manner as other costs;

(3) In the exercise of its discretion, the court may authorize disclosure to the jury of the fact that the court appointed the expert witness; and

(4) Nothing in this Code section shall limit a party in calling expert witnesses of the party's own selection.

§ 24-7-707. Expert opinion testimony in criminal proceedings

In criminal proceedings, the opinions of experts on any question of science, skill, trade, or like questions shall always be admissible; and such opinions may be given on the facts as proved by other witnesses.

CHAPTER 8. HEARSAY

ARTICLE 1. GENERAL PROVISIONS

§ 24-8-801. Definitions

As used in this chapter, the term:
(a) "Statement" means:
    (1) An oral or written assertion; or
    (2) Nonverbal conduct of a person, if it is intended by the person as an assertion.
(b) "Declarant" means a person who makes a statement.
(c) "Hearsay" means a statement, other than one made by the declarant while testifying at the trial or hearing, offered in evidence to prove the truth of the matter asserted.
(d) "Hearsay" shall be subject to the following exclusions and conditions:
    (1) Prior statement by witness.
        (A) An out-of-court statement shall not be hearsay if the declarant testifies at the trial or hearing, is subject to cross-examination concerning the statement, and the statement is admissible as a prior inconsistent statement or a prior consistent statement under Code Section 24-6-613 or is otherwise admissible under this chapter.
        (B) If a hearsay statement is admitted and the declarant does not testify at the trial or hearing, other out-of-court statements of the declarant shall be admissible for the limited use of impeaching or rehabilitating the credibility of the declarant, and not as substantive evidence, if the other statements qualify as prior inconsistent statements or prior consistent statements under Code Section 24-6-613.
        (C) A statement shall not be hearsay if the declarant testifies at the trial or hearing and is subject to cross-examination concerning the statement, and the statement is one of identification of a person made after perceiving the person; and
    (2) Admissions by party-opponent. Admissions shall not be excluded by the hearsay rule. An admission is a statement offered against a party which is:
        (A) The party's own statement, in either an individual or representative capacity;
        (B) A statement of which the party has manifested an adoption or belief in its truth;
        (C) A statement by a person authorized by the party to make a statement concerning the subject;
        (D) A statement by the party's agent or employee, but not including any agent of the state in a criminal proceeding, concerning a

matter within the scope of the agency or employment, made during the existence of the relationship; or

(E) A statement by a coconspirator of a party during the course and in furtherance of the conspiracy, including a statement made during the concealment phase of a conspiracy. A conspiracy need not be charged in order to make a statement admissible under this subparagraph.

The contents of the statement shall be considered but shall not alone be sufficient to establish the declarant's authority under subparagraph (C) of this paragraph, the agency or employment relationship and scope thereof under subparagraph (D) of this paragraph, or the existence of the conspiracy and the participation therein of the declarant and the party against whom the statement is offered under subparagraph (E) of this paragraph.

(e) "Public office" means:

(1) Every state department, agency, board, bureau, commission, division, public corporation, and authority;

(2) Every county, municipal corporation, school district, or other political subdivision of this state;

(3) Every department, agency, board, bureau, commission, authority, or similar body of each such county, municipal corporation, or other political subdivision of this state; and

(4) Every city, county, regional, or other authority established pursuant to the laws of this state.

(f) "Public official" means an elected or appointed official.

(g) "Public record" means information that is inscribed on a tangible medium or that is stored in an electronic or other medium and is retrievable in perceivable form and created in the course of the operation of a public office.

§ 24-8-802. Hearsay rule

Hearsay shall not be admissible except as provided by this article; provided, however, that if a party does not properly object to hearsay, the objection shall be deemed waived, and the hearsay evidence shall be legal evidence and admissible.

§ 24-8-803. Hearsay rule exceptions; availability of declarant immaterial

The following shall not be excluded by the hearsay rule, even though the declarant is available as a witness:

(1) Present sense impression. A statement describing or explaining an event or condition made while the declarant was perceiving the event or condition or immediately thereafter;

(2) Excited utterance. A statement relating to a startling event or condition made while the declarant was under the stress of excitement caused by the event or condition;

(3) Then existing mental, emotional, or physical condition. A statement of the declarant's then existing state of mind, emotion, sensation, or physical condition, such as intent, plan, motive, design, mental feeling, pain, and bodily health, but not including a statement of memory or belief to prove the fact remembered or believed unless such statements relate to the execution, revocation, identification, or terms of the declarant's will and not including a statement of belief as to the intent of another person;

(4) Statements for purposes of medical diagnosis or treatment. Statements made for purposes of medical diagnosis or treatment and describing medical history, or past or present symptoms, pain, or sensations, or the inception or general character of the cause or external source thereof insofar as reasonably pertinent to diagnosis or treatment;

(5) Recorded recollection. A memorandum or record concerning a matter about which a witness once had knowledge but now has insufficient recollection to enable the witness to testify fully and accurately shown to have been made or adopted by the witness when the matter was fresh in the witness's memory and to reflect that knowledge correctly. If admitted, the memorandum or record may be read into evidence but shall not itself be received as an exhibit unless offered by an adverse party;

(6) Records of regularly conducted activity. Unless the source of information or the method or circumstances of preparation indicate lack of trustworthiness and subject to the provisions of Chapter 7 of this title, a memorandum, report, record, or data compilation, in any form, of acts, events, conditions, opinions, or diagnoses, if (A) made at or near the time of the described acts, events, conditions, opinions, or diagnoses; (B) made by, or from information transmitted by, a person with personal knowledge and a business duty to report; (C) kept in the course of a regularly conducted business activity; and (D) it was the regular practice of that business activity to make the memorandum, report, record, or data compilation, all as shown by the testimony of the custodian or other qualified witness or by certification that complies with paragraph (11) or (12) of Code Section 24-9-902 or by any other statute permitting certification. The term "business" as used in this paragraph includes any business, institution, association, profession, occupation, and calling of every kind, whether or not conducted for profit. Public records and reports shall be admissible under paragraph (8) of this Code section and shall not be admissible under this paragraph;

(7) Absence of entry in records kept in accordance with paragraph (6) of this Code section. Evidence that a matter is not included in the memoranda, reports, records, or data compilations, in any form, kept in accordance with the provisions of paragraph (6) of this Code section, to prove the nonoccurrence or nonexistence of the matter, if

the matter was of a kind of which a memorandum, report, record, or data compilation was regularly made and preserved, unless the sources of information or other circumstances indicate lack of trustworthiness;

(8) Public records and reports. Except as otherwise provided by law, public records, reports, statements, or data compilations, in any form, of public offices, setting forth:

    (A) The activities of the public office;

    (B) Matters observed pursuant to duty imposed by law as to which matters there was a duty to report, excluding, however, against the accused in criminal proceedings, matters observed by police officers and other law enforcement personnel in connection with an investigation; or

    (C) In civil proceedings and against the state in criminal proceedings, factual findings resulting from an investigation made pursuant to authority granted by law, unless the sources of information or other circumstances indicate lack of trustworthiness;

(9) Records of vital statistics. Records or data compilations, in any form, of births, fetal deaths, deaths, or marriages, if the report thereof was made to a public office pursuant to requirements of law;

(10) Absence of public record or entry. To prove the absence of a record, report, statement, or data compilation, in any form, or the nonoccurrence or nonexistence of a matter of which a record, report, statement, or data compilation, in any form, was regularly made and preserved by a public office, evidence in the form of a certification in accordance with Code Section 24-9-902, or testimony, that diligent search failed to disclose the record, report, statement, or data compilation, or entry;

(11) Records of religious organizations. Statements of birth, marriages, divorces, deaths, legitimacy, ancestry, relationship by blood or marriage, or other similar facts of personal or family history, contained in a regularly kept record of a religious organization;

(12) Marriage, baptismal, and similar certificates. Statements of fact contained in a certificate that the maker performed a marriage or other ceremony or administered a sacrament, made by a clergyman, public official, or other person authorized by the rules or practices of a religious organization or by law to perform the act certified and purporting to have been issued at the time of the act or within a reasonable time thereafter;

(13) Family records. Statements of fact concerning personal or family history contained in family Bibles, genealogies, charts, engravings on rings, inscriptions on family portraits, engravings on urns, crypts, or tombstones, or the like;

(14) Records of documents affecting an interest in property. The record of a document purporting to establish or affect an interest in property, as proof of the content of the original recorded document and its

execution and delivery by each person by whom it purports to have been executed, if the record is a record of a public office and an applicable law authorizes the recording of documents of that kind in such office;

(15) Statements in documents affecting an interest in property. A statement contained in a document purporting to establish or affect an interest in property if the matter stated was relevant to the purpose of the document, unless dealings with the property since the document was made have been inconsistent with the truth of the statement or the purport of the document;

(16) Statements in ancient documents. Statements in a document in existence 20 years or more the authenticity of which is established;

(17) Market reports and commercial publications. Market quotations, tabulations, lists, directories, or other published compilations generally used and relied upon by the public or by persons in the witness's particular occupation;

(18) Learned treatises. To the extent called to the attention of an expert witness upon cross-examination, statements contained in published treatises, periodicals, or pamphlets, whether published electronically or in print, on a subject of history, medicine, or other science or art, established as a reliable authority by the testimony or admission of the witness, by other expert testimony, or by judicial notice. If admitted, the statements may be used for cross-examination of an expert witness and read into evidence but shall not be received as exhibits;

(19) Reputation concerning personal or family history. Reputation among members of a person's family by blood, adoption, or marriage or among a person's associates or in the community concerning a person's birth, adoption, marriage, divorce, death, legitimacy, relationship by blood, adoption, or marriage, ancestry, or other similar fact of the person's personal or family history;

(20) Reputation concerning boundaries or general history. Reputation in a community, arising before the controversy, as to boundaries of or customs affecting lands in the community and reputation as to events of general history important to the community or state or nation in which such lands are located;

(21) Reputation as to character. Reputation of a person's character among associates or in the community;

(22) Judgment of previous conviction. Evidence of a final judgment, entered after a trial or upon a plea of guilty but not upon a plea of nolo contendere, adjudging a person guilty of a crime punishable by death or imprisonment in excess of one year to prove any fact essential to sustain the judgment, but not including, when offered by the state in a criminal prosecution for purposes other than impeachment, judgments against persons other than the accused. The

pendency of an appeal may be shown but shall not affect admissibility; or

(23) Judgment as to personal, family, or general history or boundaries. Judgments as proof of matters of personal, family, or general history or boundaries essential to the judgment, if the same would be provable by evidence of reputation.

§ 24-8-804. Hearsay rule exceptions; declarant unavailable

(a) As used in this Code section, the term "unavailable as a witness" includes situations in which the declarant:

    (1) Is exempted by ruling of the court on the ground of privilege from testifying concerning the subject matter of the declarant's statement;

    (2) Persists in refusing to testify concerning the subject matter of the declarant's statement despite an order of the court to do so;

    (3) Testifies to a lack of memory of the subject matter of the declarant's statement;

    (4) Is unable to be present or to testify at the hearing because of death or then existing physical or mental illness or infirmity; or

    (5) Is absent from the hearing and the proponent of the statement has been unable to procure the declarant's attendance or, in the case of exceptions under paragraph (2), (3), or (4) of subsection (b) of this Code section, the declarant's attendance or testimony, by process or other reasonable means.

(b) A declarant shall not be deemed unavailable as a witness if the declarant's exemption, refusal, claim of lack of memory, inability, or absence is due to the procurement or wrongdoing of the proponent of a statement for the purpose of preventing the witness from attending or testifying.

(c) The following shall not be excluded by the hearsay rule if the declarant is unavailable as a witness:

    (1) Testimony given as a witness at another hearing of the same or a different proceeding, or in a deposition taken in compliance with law in the course of the same or another proceeding, if the party against whom the testimony is now offered, or, in a civil proceeding, a predecessor in interest, had an opportunity and similar motive to develop the testimony by direct, cross, or redirect examination. If deposition testimony is admissible under either the rules stated in Code Section 9-11-32 or this Code section, it shall be admissible at trial in accordance with the rules under which it was offered;

    (2) In a prosecution for homicide or in a civil proceeding, a statement made by a declarant while believing that his or her death was imminent, concerning the cause or circumstances of what the declarant believed to be impending death;

    (3) A statement against interest. A statement against interest is a statement:

(A) Which a reasonable person in the declarant's position would have made only if the person believed it to be true because, when made, it was so contrary to the declarant's proprietary or pecuniary interest or had so great a tendency to invalidate a claim by the declarant against another or to expose the declarant to civil or criminal liability; and

(B) Supported by corroborating circumstances that clearly indicate the trustworthiness of the statement if it is offered in a criminal case as a statement that tends to expose the declarant to criminal liability;

(4) A statement concerning the declarant's own birth, adoption, marriage, divorce, legitimacy, relationship by blood, adoption, or marriage, ancestry, or other similar fact of personal or family history, even though the declarant had no means of acquiring personal knowledge of the matter stated or a statement concerning the foregoing matters and death also of another person, if the declarant was related to the other by blood, adoption, or marriage or was so intimately associated with the other's family as to be likely to have accurate information concerning the matter declared; or

(5) A statement offered against a party that has engaged or acquiesced in wrongdoing that was intended to, and did, procure the unavailability of the declarant as a witness.

§ 24-8-805. Hearsay within hearsay

Hearsay included within hearsay shall not be excluded under the hearsay rule if each part of the combined statements conforms with an exception to the hearsay rule.

§ 24-8-806. Attacking and supporting credibility of a declarant

When a hearsay statement has been admitted in evidence, the credibility of the declarant may be attacked and, if attacked, may be supported by any evidence which would be admissible for those purposes if the declarant had testified as a witness. Evidence of a statement or conduct by the declarant at any time, inconsistent with the declarant's hearsay statement, shall not be subject to any requirement that the declarant may have been afforded an opportunity to deny or explain. If the party against whom a hearsay statement has been admitted calls the declarant as a witness, the party shall be entitled to examine the declarant on the statement as if under cross-examination.

§ 24-8-807. Residual exception

A statement not specifically covered by any law but having equivalent circumstantial guarantees of trustworthiness shall not be excluded by the hearsay rule, if the court determines that:

(1) The statement is offered as evidence of a material fact;

(2) The statement is more probative on the point for which it is offered than any other evidence which the proponent can procure through reasonable efforts; and

(3) The general purposes of the rules of evidence and the interests of justice will best be served by admission of the statement into evidence.

However, a statement may not be admitted under this Code section unless the proponent of it makes known to the adverse party, sufficiently in advance of the trial or hearing to provide the adverse party with a fair opportunity to prepare to meet it, the proponent's intention to offer the statement and the particulars of it, including the name and address of the declarant.

ARTICLE 2. ADMISSIONS AND CONFESSIONS

§ 24-8-820. Testimony as to child's description of sexual contact or physical abuse

A statement made by a child younger than 16 years of age describing any act of sexual contact or physical abuse performed with or on such child by another or with or on another in the presence of such child shall be admissible in evidence by the testimony of the person to whom made if the proponent of such statement provides notice to the adverse party prior to trial of the intention to use such out-of-court statement and such child testifies at the trial, unless the adverse party forfeits or waives such child's testimony as provided in this title, and, at the time of the testimony regarding the out-of-court statements, the person to whom the child made such statement is subject to cross-examination regarding the out-of-court statements.

§ 24-8-821. Admissions in pleadings

Without offering the same in evidence, either party may avail himself or herself of allegations or admissions made in the pleadings of the other.

§ 24-8-822. Right to have whole conversation heard

When an admission is given in evidence by one party, it shall be the right of the other party to have the whole admission and all the conversation connected therewith admitted into evidence.

§ 24-8-823. Admissions and confessions received with care; no conviction on uncorroborated confession

All admissions shall be scanned with care, and confessions of guilt shall be received with great caution. A confession alone, uncorroborated by any other evidence, shall not justify a conviction.

§ 24-8-824. Only voluntary confessions admissible

To make a confession admissible, it shall have been made voluntarily, without being induced by another by the slightest hope of benefit or remotest fear of injury.

§ 24-8-825. Confessions under spiritual exhortation, promise of secrecy, or collateral benefit admissible

The fact that a confession has been made under a spiritual exhortation, a promise of secrecy, or a promise of collateral benefit shall not exclude it.

§ 24-8-826. Medical reports in narrative form

(a) Upon the trial of any civil proceeding involving injury or disease, any medical report in narrative form which has been signed and dated by an examining or treating licensed physician, dentist, orthodontist, podiatrist, physical or occupational therapist, doctor of chiropractic, psychologist, advanced practice registered nurse, social worker, professional counselor, or marriage and family therapist shall be admissible and received in evidence insofar as it purports to represent the history, examination, diagnosis, treatment, prognosis, or interpretation of tests or examinations, including the basis therefor, by the person signing the report, the same as if that person were present at trial and testifying as a witness; provided, however, that such report and notice of intention to introduce such report shall first be provided to the adverse party at least 60 days prior to trial. A statement of the qualifications of the person signing such report may be included as part of the basis for providing the information contained therein, and the opinion of the person signing the report with regard to the etiology of the injury or disease may be included as part of the diagnosis. Any adverse party may object to the admissibility of any portion of the report, other than on the ground that it is hearsay, within 15 days of being provided with the report. Further, any adverse party shall have the right to cross-examine the person signing the report and provide rebuttal testimony. The party tendering the report may also introduce testimony of the person signing the report for the purpose of supplementing the report or otherwise.

(b) The medical narrative shall be presented to the jury as depositions are presented to the jury and shall not go out with the jury as documentary evidence.

CHAPTER 9. AUTHENTICATION AND IDENTIFICATION

ARTICLE 1. GENERAL PROVISIONS

§ 24-9-901. Requirement of authentication or identification

(a) The requirement of authentication or identification as a condition precedent to admissibility shall be satisfied by evidence sufficient to support a finding that the matter in question is what its proponent claims.

(b) By way of illustration only, and not by way of limitation, the following are examples of authentication or identification conforming with the requirements of this Code section:

  (1) Testimony of a witness with knowledge that a matter is what it is claimed to be; → *strongest method*

  (2) Nonexpert opinion as to the genuineness of handwriting, based upon familiarity not acquired for purposes of the litigation;

  (3) Comparison by the trier of fact or by expert witnesses with specimens which have been authenticated. Such specimens shall be furnished to the opposite party no later than ten days prior to trial;

  (4) Appearance, contents, substance, internal patterns, or other distinctive characteristics, taken in conjunction with circumstances;

  (5) Identification of a voice, whether heard firsthand or through mechanical or electronic transmission or recording, by opinion based upon hearing the voice at any time under circumstances connecting it with the alleged speaker;

  (6) Telephone conversations, by evidence that a call was made to the number assigned at the time by a telephone service provider to a particular person or business, if:

    (A) In the case of a person, circumstances, including self-identification, show the person answering to be the one called; or

    (B) In the case of a business, the call was made to a place of business and the conversation related to business reasonably transacted over the telephone;

  (7) Evidence that a document authorized by law to be recorded or filed and in fact recorded or filed in a public office or a purported public record, report, statement, or data compilation, in any form, is from the public office where items of this nature are kept;

  (8) Evidence that a document or data compilation, in any form:

    (A) Is in such condition as to create no suspicion concerning its authenticity;

    (B) Was in a place where it, if authentic, would likely be; and

    (C) Has been in existence 20 years or more at the time it is offered;

  (9) Evidence describing a process or system used to produce a result and showing that the process or system produces an accurate result; or

  (10) Any method of authentication or identification provided by law.

may include voice communications + computer printout.

[handwritten at top: → can still object on hearsay, relevance, or right to confrontation grounds]

§ 24-9-902. Self-authentication

Extrinsic evidence of authenticity as a condition precedent to admissibility shall not be required with respect to the following:

(1) A document bearing a seal purporting to be that of the United States or of any state, district, commonwealth, territory, or insular possession thereof or the Panama Canal Zone or the Trust Territory of the Pacific Islands or of a political subdivision, department, officer, or agency thereof or of a municipal corporation of this state and bearing a signature purporting to be an attestation or execution;

(2) A document purporting to bear the signature in the official capacity of an officer or employee of any entity included in paragraph (1) of this Code section having no seal, if a public officer having a seal and having official duties in the district or political subdivision of the officer or employee certifies under seal that the signer has the official capacity and that the signature is genuine;

(3) A document purporting to be executed or attested in an official capacity by a person authorized by the laws of a foreign country to make such execution or attestation and accompanied by a final certification as to the genuineness of the signature, official position of the executing or attesting person, or of any foreign official whose certificate of genuineness of signature and official position relates to such execution or attestation or is in a chain of certificates of genuineness of signature and official position relating to such execution or attestation. A final certification may be made by a secretary of embassy or legation, consul general, consul, vice consul, or consular agent of the United States or a diplomatic or consular official of the foreign country assigned or accredited to the United States. If reasonable opportunity has been given to all parties to investigate the authenticity and accuracy of official documents, the court may, for good cause shown, order that such documents be treated as presumptively authentic without final certification or permit such documents to be evidenced by an attested summary with or without final certification;

(4) A duplicate of an official record or report or entry therein or of a document authorized by law to be recorded or filed and actually recorded or filed in a public office, including data compilations in any form, certified as correct by the custodian or other person authorized to make the certification by certificate complying with paragraph (1), (2), or (3) of this Code section or complying with any law of the United States or of this state, including Code Section 24-9-920;

(5) Books, pamphlets, or other publications purporting to be issued by a public office;

(6) Printed materials purporting to be newspapers or periodicals;

(7) Inscriptions, signs, tags, or labels purporting to have been affixed in the course of business and indicating ownership, control, or origin;

(8) Documents accompanied by a certificate of acknowledgment executed in the manner provided by law by a notary public or other officer authorized by law to take acknowledgments;

(9) Commercial paper, signatures thereon, and documents relating thereto to the extent provided by general commercial law;

(10) Any signature, document, or other matter declared by any law of the United States or of this state to be presumptively or prima facie genuine or authentic;

(11) The original or a duplicate of a domestic record of regularly conducted activity that would be admissible under paragraph (6) of Code Section 24-8-803 if accompanied by a written declaration of its custodian or other qualified person certifying that the record:

    (A) Was made at or near the time of the occurrence of the matters set forth by, or from information transmitted by, a person with knowledge of such matters;

    (B) Was kept in the course of the regularly conducted activity; and

    (C) Was made by the regularly conducted activity as a regular practice.

A party intending to offer a record into evidence under this paragraph shall provide written notice of such intention to all adverse parties and shall make the record and declaration available for inspection sufficiently in advance of their offer into evidence to provide an adverse party with a fair opportunity to challenge such record and declaration; or

(12) In a civil proceeding, the original or a duplicate of a foreign record of regularly conducted activity that would be admissible under paragraph (6) of Code Section 24-8-803 if accompanied by a written declaration by its custodian or other qualified person certifying that the record:

    (A) Was made at or near the time of the occurrence of the matters set forth by, or from information transmitted by, a person with knowledge of those matters;

    (B) Was kept in the course of the regularly conducted activity; and

    (C) Was made by the regularly conducted activity as a regular practice.

(b) The declaration shall be signed in a manner that, if falsely made, would subject the maker to criminal penalty under the laws of the country where the declaration is signed. A party intending to offer a record into evidence under this paragraph shall provide written notice of such intention to all adverse parties and shall make the record and declaration available for inspection sufficiently in advance of their offer into evidence to provide an adverse party with a fair opportunity to challenge such record and declaration.

§ 24-9-903. Subscribing witness's testimony

The testimony of a subscribing witness shall not be necessary to authenticate a writing unless required by the laws of the jurisdiction whose laws govern the validity of the writing.

§ 24-9-904. Definitions

As used in this article, the term:
 (1) "Public office" shall have the same meaning as set forth in Code Section 24-8-801.
 (2) "Public officer" means any person appointed or elected to be the head of any entity included in paragraph (1) of Code Section 24-9-902.
 (3) "Telephone service provider" shall have the same meaning as "voice service provider" as set forth in Code Section 46-5-231.

ARTICLE 2. SPECIFIC TYPES OF RECORDS AND EVIDENCE

§ 24-9-920. Authentication of Georgia state and county records

The certificate or attestation of any public officer either of this state or any county thereof or any clerk or keeper of county, consolidated government, or municipal records in this state shall give sufficient validity or authenticity to any copy or transcript of any record, document, paper or file, or other matter or thing in such public officer's respective office, or pertaining thereto, to admit the same in evidence.

§ 24-9-921. Identification of medical bills; expert witness unnecessary

(a) Upon the trial of any civil proceeding involving injury or disease, the patient or the member of his or her family or other person responsible for the care of the patient shall be a competent witness to identify bills for expenses incurred in the treatment of the patient upon a showing by such a witness that the expenses were incurred in connection with the treatment of the injury, disease, or disability involved in the subject of litigation at trial and that the bills were received from:
 (1) A hospital;
 (2) An ambulance service;
 (3) A pharmacy, drugstore, or supplier of therapeutic or orthopedic devices; or
 (4) A licensed practicing physician, dentist, orthodontist, podiatrist, physical or occupational therapist, doctor of chiropractic, psychologist, advanced practice registered nurse, social worker, professional counselor, or marriage and family therapist.
(b) Such items of evidence need not be identified by the one who submits the bill, and it shall not be necessary for an expert witness to testify that the charges were reasonable and necessary. However, nothing in this Code

section shall be construed to limit the right of a thorough and sifting cross-examination as to such items of evidence.

§ 24-9-922. Proof of laws, records, nonjudicial records, or books of other states, territories, or possessions; full faith and credit

The acts of the legislature of any other state, territory, or possession of the United States, the records and judicial proceedings of any court of any such state, territory, or possession, and the nonjudicial records or books kept in the public offices in any such state, territory, or possession, if properly authenticated, shall have the same full faith and credit in every court within this state as they have by law or usage in the courts of such state, territory, or possession from which they are taken.

§ 24-9-923. Authentication of photographs, motion pictures, video recordings, and audio recordings when witness unavailable

(a) As used in this Code section, the term "unavailability of a witness" includes situations in which the authenticating witness:
  (1) Is exempted by ruling of the court on the ground of privilege from testifying concerning the subject matter of the authentication;
  (2) Persists in refusing to testify concerning the subject matter of the authentication despite an order of the court to do so;
  (3) Testifies to a lack of memory of the subject matter of the authentication;
  (4) Is unable to be present or to testify at the hearing because of death or then existing physical or mental illness or infirmity; or
  (5) Is absent from the hearing and the proponent of the authentication has been unable to procure the attendance of the authenticating witness by process or other reasonable means.
  An authenticating witness shall not be deemed unavailable as a witness if his or her exemption, refusal, claim of lack of memory, inability, or absence is due to the procurement or wrongdoing of the proponent of an authentication for the purpose of preventing the witness from attending or testifying.

(b) Subject to any other valid objection, photographs, motion pictures, video recordings, and audio recordings shall be admissible in evidence when necessitated by the unavailability of a witness who can provide personal authentication and when the court determines, based on competent evidence presented to the court, that such items tend to show reliably the fact or facts for which the items are offered.

(c) Subject to any other valid objection, photographs, motion pictures, video recordings, and audio recordings produced at a time when the device producing the items was not being operated by an individual person or was not under the personal control or in the presence of an individual operator shall be admissible in evidence when the court determines, based on competent evidence presented to the court, that such items tend to show reliably the fact or facts for which the items are offered, provided that, prior to the admission of such evidence, the date and time of such photograph, motion picture, or video recording shall be contained on such evidence, and such date and time shall be shown to have been made contemporaneously with the events depicted in such photograph, motion picture, or video recording.

(d) This Code section shall not be the exclusive method of introduction into evidence of photographs, motion pictures, video recordings, and audio recordings but shall be supplementary to any other law and lawful methods existing in this state.

§ 24-9-924. Admissibility of records of Department of Driver Services; admissibility of computer transmitted records

(a) Any court may receive and use as evidence in any proceeding information otherwise admissible from the records of the Department of Public Safety or the Department of Driver Services obtained from any terminal lawfully connected to the Georgia Crime Information Center without the need for additional certification of such records.

(b) Any court may receive and use as evidence for the purpose of imposing a sentence in any criminal proceeding information otherwise admissible from the records of the Department of Driver Services obtained from a request made in accordance with a contract with the Georgia Technology Authority for immediate on-line electronic furnishing of information.

CHAPTER 10. BEST EVIDENCE RULE

§ 24-10-1001. Definitions

As used in this chapter, the term:

    (1) "Writing" or "recording" means letters, words, or numbers, or their equivalent, set down by handwriting, typewriting, printing, photostating, magnetic impulse, or mechanical or electronic recording or other form of data compilation.

    (2) "Photograph" includes still photographs, X-ray films, video recordings, and motion pictures.

    (3) "Original" means the writing or recording itself or any counterpart intended to have the same effect by a person executing or issuing it. An original of a photograph includes the negative or any print therefrom. If data are stored in a computer or similar device, any printout or other output readable by sight, shown to reflect the data accurately, is an original.

    (4) "Duplicate" means a counterpart produced by the same impression as the original or from the same matrix or by means of photography, including enlargements and miniatures, or by mechanical or

electronic rerecording, chemical reproduction, or other equivalent techniques which accurately reproduce the original.

(5) "Public record" shall have the same meaning as set forth in Code Section 24-8-801.

§ 24-10-1002. Requirement of original

To prove the contents of a writing, recording, or photograph, the original writing, recording, or photograph shall be required.

§ 24-10-1003. Admissibility of duplicates

A duplicate shall be admissible to the same extent as an original unless:

(1) A genuine question is raised as to the authenticity of the original; or

(2) A circumstance exists where it would be unfair to admit the duplicate in lieu of the original.

§ 24-10-1004. Admissibility of other evidence of contents of a writing, recording, or photograph

The original shall not be required and other evidence of the contents of a writing, recording, or photograph shall be admissible if:

(1) All originals are lost or have been destroyed, unless the proponent lost or destroyed them in bad faith;

(2) No original can be obtained by any available judicial process or procedure;

(3) At a time when an original was under the control of the party against whom offered, that party was put on notice, by the pleadings or otherwise, that the contents would be a subject of proof at the hearing, and that party does not produce the original at the hearing; or

(4) The writing, recording, or photograph is not closely related to a controlling issue.

§ 24-10-1005. Public records

The contents of a public record, or of a document authorized to be recorded or filed and actually recorded or filed, including data compilations in any form, if otherwise admissible, may be proved by duplicate, certified as correct in accordance with Code Section 24-9-902 or Code Section 24-9-920 or testified to be correct by a witness who has compared it with the original. If a duplicate which complies with this Code section cannot be obtained by the exercise of reasonable diligence, then other evidence of the contents may be given.

§ 24-10-1006. Summaries

The contents of otherwise admissible voluminous writings, recordings, or photographs which cannot conveniently be examined in court may be presented in the form of a chart, summary, or calculation. The originals, or duplicates, shall be made available for examination or copying, or both, by other parties at a reasonable time and place. The court may order that the contents of such writings, recordings, or photographs be produced in court.

§ 24-10-1007. Testimony or written admission of party

The contents of writings, recordings, or photographs may be proved by the testimony or deposition of the party against whom offered or by that party's written admission, without accounting for the nonproduction of the original.

§ 24-10-1008. Functions of court and jury

When the admissibility of other evidence of the contents of writings, recordings, or photographs under the rules of evidence depends upon the fulfillment of a condition of fact, the question of whether the condition has been fulfilled is ordinarily for the court to determine in accordance with the provisions of Code Section 24-1-104; provided, however, that when an issue is raised as to:
>(1) Whether the asserted writing, recording, or photograph ever existed;
>(2) Whether another writing, recording, or photograph produced at the trial is the original; or
>(3) Whether other evidence of the contents correctly reflects the contents,

the issue is for the trier of fact to determine as in the case of other issues of fact.

CHAPTER 11. ESTABLISHMENT OF LOST RECORDS

ARTICLE 1. PUBLIC RECORDS

§ 24-11-1. Definitions

As used in this chapter, the term:
>(1) "Custodian" means the person charged with the duty of maintaining public records.
>(2) "Duplicate" means a counterpart which accurately reproduces the original.
>(3) "Public record" shall have the same meaning as set forth in Code Section 24-8-801.

§ 24-11-2. Establishment of lost records

(a) Where any original public records have been lost, mutilated, stolen, or destroyed, the custodian may establish duplicates in accordance with the provisions of this article. When such public records are established by duplicates, they shall have all of the effect in evidence as the original records would have had.

(b) The custodian of the lost, mutilated, stolen, or destroyed public records shall bring a petition to establish such records in the superior court of the county in which the public records were located.

(c) The petition shall set forth the fact that some portion of the public records has been lost, mutilated, stolen, or destroyed, specifying as nearly as may be possible the books or parts of the books in which those records existed, and shall pray for the establishment of such records.

§ 24-11-3. Appointment of auditor; hearing; establishment of duplicates

(a) The court shall either appoint an auditor for such petition in accordance with Chapter 7 of Title 9 or shall conduct a hearing on the petition. If an auditor is appointed, the provisions of Code Sections 9-7-1 through 9-7-16 and Code Section 9-7-21 shall apply to such proceedings. An auditor shall receive compensation for services rendered as may be allowed by the court, to be paid out of the funds of the office of the custodian whose records were lost, mutilated, stolen, or destroyed.

(b) If the court hears the petition, after receiving evidence, the court shall determine whether the purported duplicate is, in fact, the same as the original record which has been lost, mutilated, stolen, or destroyed, and it shall be discretionary with the court to order the whole or any part of such records established. The court shall give precedence to a petition filed pursuant to this article and hear the petition as speedily as possible.

(c) The duplicates which are established pursuant to this Code section, as nearly as may be possible, shall specify and conform to the original book and pages of the same on which they originally existed.

ARTICLE 2. PRIVATE PAPERS

§ 24-11-20. Establishment of lost office papers

(a) Upon the loss of any original pleading, declaration, bill of indictment, special presentment, accusation, or other office paper, a duplicate may be established instanter on motion.

(b) As used in this article, the term "office paper" means the instrument upon which a proceeding has been brought after the case has gone to trial.

§ 24-11-21. Summary establishment of lost or destroyed evidence of indebtedness in probate court -- Petition; service of notice; hearing and decision; recordation; appeal to superior court

(a) The owner, agent of the owner, or legal representative of the owner of any bond, bill, note, draft, check, or other evidence of indebtedness which has been lost or destroyed may establish a duplicate of the same in a summary manner by filing a petition with the judge of the probate court of the county of the residence of the alleged debtor or maker, if he or she is a resident of this state; and the judge of the probate court shall be deemed a judicial officer for the purpose of this Code section. The petition shall be sworn to by the party applying and shall contain as full and accurate a description as possible of the lost paper, of the loss and mode of loss, and of the inability to find the same and why, along with a prayer for the establishment of a duplicate setting forth the duplicate desired to be established.

(b) Upon the filing of a petition, the judge shall issue a citation or notice to the alleged debtor or maker requiring the debtor or maker to appear at a day not more than ten days distant and show cause, if he or she has any, why the duplicate should not be established in lieu of the lost original. The citation or notice shall be personally served in the manner provided in Code Section 9-11-4 at least five days before the time of the hearing.

(c) If no successful defense is made at the time and place appointed, the judge shall proceed to establish, by an order entered on the petition, the duplicate so prayed to be established, which shall have all the effect of the original. The petition, notice, and order shall be entered in a book of record specially prepared for this purpose.

(d) If the debtor or maker files a defense under oath to the effect that the original never existed as claimed, the judge shall decide the case, after giving the parties time for preparation and hearing, not to exceed 20 days. If the judge's decision is in favor of the applicant and no appeal is entered as provided in subsection (e) of this Code section, the decision shall be entered on the petition, and the duplicate so established shall have the same effect as an original. If the judge's decision is in favor of the alleged debtor or maker, the judge shall also enter his or her decision on the petition. In all cases, the proceedings shall be recorded as provided in subsection (c) of this Code section.

(e) Except as provided in Article 6 of Chapter 9 of Title 15, if either party to the proceedings provided for in this Code section is dissatisfied, such party may appeal upon giving the usual bond and security for costs, as in cases of appeal from the probate court to the superior court. The appeal shall be tried in the superior court from all the pleadings and proceedings as were before the judge of the probate court. In the superior court, the case shall be tried and determined as provided in Code Sections 24-11-23 through 24-11-26.

(f) This Code section shall not apply to evidences of indebtedness to which Title 11, the "Uniform Commercial Code," is applicable.

§ 24-11-22. Summary establishment of lost or destroyed evidence of indebtedness in probate court -- Service of nonresidents; effect

When the person alleged to be a debtor or maker of a lost or destroyed paper as set forth in Code Section 24-11-21 does not reside in this state, the alleged debtor or maker may be made a party to the proceedings by publication, in a newspaper to be designated by the judge of the probate court, twice a month for two months. When the person has been made a party, this article shall apply in his or her case.

§ 24-11-23. Establishment of lost or destroyed paper in superior court -- Petition and affidavit; issuance and service of rule nisi

(a) The owner of a lost or destroyed paper which is not an office paper, as defined in Code Section 24-11-20, who desires to establish such paper shall present to the clerk of the superior court of the county where the maker of the paper resides, if the maker is a resident of this state, a petition in writing, together with a duplicate, in substance, of the paper lost or destroyed, as nearly as he or she can recollect, which duplicate shall be sworn to by the petitioner, the petitioner's agent, or the petitioner's attorney.

(b) The clerk shall issue a rule nisi in the name of the judge of the superior court calling upon the opposite party to show cause, if he or she has any, why the duplicate sworn to should not be established in lieu of the lost or destroyed original. If the respondent is found in this state, the rule nisi shall be served personally upon the respondent in the manner provided by Code Section 9-11-4 at least 20 days before the sitting of the court to which the rule nisi is made returnable. If the respondent cannot be found in this state, the rule nisi shall be served upon the respondent by publication in the manner provided in Code Section 9-11-4 before the final hearing of the rule nisi.

§ 24-11-24. Establishment of lost or destroyed paper in superior court -- When continuance granted

In a proceeding to establish lost papers under Code Section 24-11-23, no continuance shall be granted unless it appears reasonable and just to the court; nor shall a continuance be allowed to the same party more than once, except for providential cause.

§ 24-11-25. Establishment of lost or destroyed paper

When a rule nisi has been served as provided in Code Section 24-11-23, the court shall grant a rule absolute establishing the duplicate of the lost or destroyed paper sworn to, unless good and sufficient cause is shown why the rule absolute should not be granted.

§ 24-11-26. Establishment of lost or destroyed paper -- Furnishing of certified endorsement of copy

When the duplicate of the lost or destroyed paper is established, the clerk of the court in which it is done shall furnish the duplicate to the party who had it established, with a certified endorsement thereon of the day and term of the court when the rule absolute was granted, provided all costs of the proceeding have been paid.

§ 24-11-27. Procedure as to action on lost or destroyed note, bill, bond, or other instrument

(a) If the paper which has been lost or destroyed is a note, bill, bond, or other instrument upon which a proceeding may be brought, the owner may institute a proceeding thereon as soon as the rule nisi has been issued as provided for in Code Section 24-11-23. The complaint shall set forth that the paper upon which the proceeding is based is lost or destroyed. In no case shall a judgment be entered in the proceeding until it is determined whether the application to establish the paper is granted or not. If the application is granted, then judgment shall be entered as in other proceedings.

(b) In a proceeding as provided for in subsection (a) of this Code section, production of the paper upon which the proceeding is based shall not be demanded until the time for rendition of judgment in the proceeding; at that time, if the plaintiff produces a duplicate of the paper with a certified endorsement thereon by the clerk of the court in which it was established, as provided in Code Section 24-11-26, it shall be taken and considered as the original.

(c) This Code section shall not apply to instruments to which Title 11, the "Uniform Commercial Code," is applicable.

§ 24-11-28. Joinder of additional party defendants in proceedings to establish lost or destroyed papers

In all proceedings for the purpose of establishing any lost or destroyed paper other than an office paper, as defined in Code Section 24-11-20, any person whose interest will be affected by the establishment of the lost paper shall, upon motion, by order of the court, be made a party respondent in the proceeding and shall be allowed all the rights of defense against the establishment of the paper as fully as if he or she was the maker of the lost paper.

§ 24-11-29. Applicability of article

Other than Code Section 24-11-20, this article shall not apply to lost or destroyed papers to which Title 11, the "Uniform Commercial Code," is applicable.

CHAPTER 12. MEDICAL AND OTHER CONFIDENTIAL INFORMATION

ARTICLE 1. RELEASE OF MEDICAL INFORMATION AND CONFIDENTIALITY OF RAW RESEARCH DATA

§ 24-12-1. When medical information may be released by physician, hospital, health care facility, or pharmacist; immunity from liability; waiver of privilege; psychiatrists and hospitals excepted

(a) No physician licensed under Chapter 34 of Title 43 and no hospital or health care facility, including those operated by an agency or bureau of this state or other governmental unit, shall be required to release any medical information concerning a patient except to the Department of Public Health, its divisions, agents, or successors when required in the administration of public health programs pursuant to Code Section 31-12-2 and where authorized or required by law, statute, or lawful regulation; or on written authorization or other waiver by the patient, or by his or her parents or duly appointed guardian ad litem in the case of a minor, or on appropriate court order or subpoena; provided, however, that any physician, hospital, or health care facility releasing information under written authorization or other waiver by the patient, or by his or her parents or guardian ad litem in the case of a minor, or pursuant to law, statute, or lawful regulation, or under court order or subpoena shall not be liable to the patient or any other person; provided, further, that the privilege shall be waived to the extent that the patient places his or her care and treatment or the nature and extent of his or her injuries at issue in any judicial proceeding. This Code section shall not apply to psychiatrists or to hospitals in which the patient is being or has been treated solely for mental illness.

(b) No pharmacist licensed under Chapter 4 of Title 26 shall be required to release any medical information concerning a patient except on written authorization or other waiver by the patient, or by his or her parents or duly appointed guardian ad litem in the case of a minor, or upon appropriate court order or subpoena; provided, however, that any pharmacist releasing information under written authorization or other waiver by the patient, or by his or her parents or duly appointed guardian ad litem in the case of a minor, or upon appropriate court order or subpoena shall not be liable to the patient or any other person; provided, further, that the privilege shall be waived to the extent that the patient places his or her care and treatment or the nature and extent of his or her injuries at issue in any judicial proceeding.

§ 24-12-2. Confidentiality of raw research data

(a) The General Assembly finds and declares that protecting the confidentiality of research data from disclosure in judicial and administrative proceedings is essential to safeguarding the integrity of research in this state, guaranteeing the privacy of individuals who participate in research projects, and ensuring the continuation of research in science, medicine, and other fields that benefits the citizens and institutions of Georgia and other states. The protection of such research data has more than local significance, is of equal importance to all citizens of this state, is of state-wide concern, and consequently is properly a matter for regulation under the police power of this state.

(b) As used in this Code section, the term "confidential raw research data" means medical information, interview responses, reports, statements, memoranda, or other data relating to the condition, treatment, or characteristics of any person which are gathered by or provided to a researcher:

  (1) In support of a research study approved by an appropriate research oversight committee of a hospital, health care facility, or educational institution; and

  (2) With the objective to develop, study, or report aggregate or anonymous information not intended to be used in any way in which the identity of an individual is material to the results.

  The term shall not include published compilations of the raw research data created by the researcher or the researcher's published summaries, findings, analyses, or conclusions related to the research study.

(c) Confidential raw research data in a researcher's possession shall not be subject to subpoena, otherwise discoverable, or deemed admissible as evidence in any judicial or administrative proceeding in any court except as otherwise provided in subsection (d) of this Code section.

(d) Confidential raw research data may be released, disclosed, subject to subpoena, otherwise discoverable, or deemed admissible as evidence in a judicial or administrative proceeding as follows:

  (1) Confidential raw research data related to a person may be disclosed to that person or to another person on such person's behalf where the authority is otherwise specifically provided by law;

  (2) Confidential raw research data related to a person may be disclosed to any person or legal entity designated to receive that information when that designation is made in writing by the research participant or where a designation is made in writing by a person authorized by law to act for the participant;

  (3) Confidential raw research data related to a person may be disclosed to any agency or department of the federal government, this state, or any political subdivision of this state if such data are required by law or regulation to be reported to such agency or department;

(4) Confidential raw research data may be disclosed in any proceeding in which a party was a participant, researcher, or sponsor in the underlying research study, including, but not limited to, any judicial or administrative proceeding in which a research participant places his or her care, treatment, injuries, insurance coverage, or benefit plan coverage at issue; provided, however, that the identity of any research participant other than the party to the judicial or administrative proceeding shall not be disclosed, unless the researcher or sponsor is a defendant in such proceeding;

(5) Confidential raw research data may be disclosed in any judicial or administrative proceeding in which the researcher has either volunteered to testify or has been hired to testify as an expert by one of the parties to such proceeding; and

(6) In a criminal proceeding, the court shall order the production of confidential raw research data if the data are relevant to any issue in the proceeding, impose appropriate safeguards against unauthorized disclosure of the data, and admit confidential raw research data into evidence if the data are material to the defense or prosecution.

(e) Nothing in this Code section shall be construed to permit, require, or prohibit the disclosure of confidential raw research data in any setting other than a judicial or administrative proceeding that is governed by the requirements of this title.

(f) Any disclosure of confidential raw research data authorized or required by this Code section or any other law shall in no way destroy the confidential nature of that data except for the purpose for which the authorized or required disclosure is made.

ARTICLE 2. CONFIDENTIALITY OF MEDICAL INFORMATION

§ 24-12-10. Definitions

As used in this article, the term:

(1) "Confidential or privileged" means the protection afforded by law from unauthorized disclosure, whether the protection is afforded by law as developed and applied by the courts, by statute or lawful regulations, or by the requirements of the Constitutions of the State of Georgia or the United States. The term "confidential or privileged" also includes protection afforded by law from compulsory process or testimony.

(2) "Disclosure" means the act of transmitting or communicating medical matter to a person who would not otherwise have access thereto.

(3) "Health care facility" means any institution or place in which health care is rendered to persons, which health care includes, but is not limited to, medical, psychiatric, acute, intermediate, rehabilitative, and long-term care.

(4) "Laws requiring disclosure" means laws and statutes of the State of Georgia and of the United States and lawful regulations issued by any department or agency of the State of Georgia or of the United States which require the review, analysis, or use of medical matter by persons not originally having authorized access thereto. The term "laws requiring disclosure" also includes any authorized practice of disclosure for purposes of evaluating claims for reimbursement for charges or expenses under any public or private reimbursement or insurance program.

(5) "Limited consent to disclosure" means proper authorization given by or on behalf of a person entitled to protection from disclosure of medical matter and given for a specific purpose related to such person's health or related to such person's application for insurance or like benefits.

(6) "Medical matter" means information respecting the medical or psychiatric condition, including without limitation the physical and the mental condition, of a natural person or persons, however recorded, obtained, or communicated.

(7) "Nurse" means a person authorized by license issued under Chapter 26 of Title 43 as a registered professional nurse or licensed practical nurse to practice nursing.

(8) "Physician" means any person lawfully licensed in this state to practice medicine and surgery pursuant to Chapter 34 of Title 43.

§ 24-12-11. Disclosure of medical records -- Effect on confidential or privileged character thereof

The disclosure of confidential or privileged medical matter constituting all or part of a record kept by a health care facility, a nurse, or a physician, pursuant to laws requiring disclosure or pursuant to limited consent to disclosure, shall not serve to destroy or in any way abridge the confidential or privileged character thereof, except for the purpose for which such disclosure is made.

§ 24-12-12. Disclosure of medical records -- Use of medical matter disclosed

Persons to whom confidential or privileged medical matter is disclosed in the circumstances described in Code Section 24-12-11 shall utilize such matter only in connection with the purpose or purposes of such disclosure and thereafter shall keep such matter in confidence. However, nothing in this article shall prohibit the use of such matter where otherwise authorized by law.

§ 24-12-13. Disclosure of medical records -- Immunity from liability

Any person, corporation, authority, or other legal entity acting in good faith shall be immune from liability for the transmission, receipt, or use of medical matter disclosed pursuant to laws requiring disclosure or pursuant to limited consent to disclosure.

§ 24-12-14. Disclosure of medical records -- Use for educational purposes not precluded

Nothing in this article shall be construed to prevent the customary and usual audit, discussion, and presentation of cases in connection with medical and public education.

ARTICLE 3. AIDS INFORMATION

§ 24-12-20. Confidential nature of AIDS information

AIDS confidential information as defined in Code Section 31-22-9.1 and disclosed or discovered within the patient-physician relationship shall be confidential and shall not be disclosed except as otherwise provided in Code Section 24-12-21.

§ 24-12-21. Disclosure of AIDS confidential information

(a) Any term used in this Code section and defined in Code Section 31-22-9.1 shall have the meaning provided for such term in Code Section 31-22-9.1.
(b) Except as otherwise provided in this Code section:
   (1) No person or legal entity which receives AIDS confidential information pursuant to this Code section or which is responsible for recording, reporting, or maintaining AIDS confidential information shall:
      (A) Intentionally or knowingly disclose that information to another person or legal entity; or
      (B) Be compelled by subpoena, court order, or other judicial process to disclose that information to another person or legal entity; and
   (2) No person or legal entity which receives AIDS confidential information which that person or legal entity knows was disclosed in violation of paragraph (1) of this subsection shall:
      (A) Intentionally or knowingly disclose that information to another person or legal entity; or
      (B) Be compelled by subpoena, court order, or other judicial process to disclose that information to another person or legal entity.
(c) AIDS confidential information shall be disclosed to the person identified by that information or, if that person is an incompetent person, to that person's legal guardian. AIDS confidential information may be disclosed to such person's parent or legal guardian if that person is a minor.
(d) AIDS confidential information shall be disclosed to any person or legal entity designated to receive that information when that designation is made in writing by the person identified by that information or, if that

person is a minor or incompetent person, by that person's parent or legal guardian.

(e) AIDS confidential information shall be disclosed to any agency or department of the federal government, this state, or any political subdivision of this state if that information is authorized or required by law to be reported to that agency or department.

(f) The results of an HIV test shall be disclosed to the person, or that person's designated representative, who ordered such tests of the body fluids or tissue of another person.

(g) When the patient of a physician has been determined to be infected with HIV and that patient's physician reasonably believes that the spouse or sexual partner or any child of the patient, spouse, or sexual partner is a person at risk of being infected with HIV by that patient, the physician may disclose to that spouse, sexual partner, or child that the patient has been determined to be infected with HIV, after first attempting to notify the patient that such disclosure is going to be made.

(h)

    (1) An administrator of an institution licensed as a hospital by the Department of Community Health or a physician having a patient who has been determined to be infected with HIV may disclose to the Department of Public Health:
        (A) The name and address of that patient;
        (B) That such patient has been determined to be infected with HIV; and
        (C) The name and address of any other person whom the disclosing physician or administrator reasonably believes to be a person at risk of being infected with HIV by that patient.

    (2) When mandatory and nonanonymous reporting of confirmed positive HIV tests to the Department of Public Health is determined by that department to be reasonably necessary, that department shall establish by regulation a date on and after which such reporting shall be required. On and after the date so established, each health care provider, health care facility, or any other person or legal entity which orders an HIV test for another person shall report to the Department of Public Health the name and address of any person thereby determined to be infected with HIV. No such report shall be made regarding any confirmed positive HIV test provided at any anonymous HIV test site operated by or on behalf of the Department of Public Health.

    (3) The Department of Public Health may disclose that a person has been reported, under paragraph (1) or (2) of this subsection, to have been determined to be infected with HIV to the board of health of the county in which that person resides or is located if reasonably necessary to protect the health and safety of that person or other persons who may have come in contact with the body fluids of the HIV infected person. The Department of Public Health or county

board of health to which information is disclosed pursuant to this paragraph or paragraph (1) or (2) of this subsection:

    (A) May contact any person named in such disclosure as having been determined to be an HIV infected person for the purpose of counseling that person and requesting therefrom the name of any other person who may be a person at risk of being infected with HIV by that HIV infected person;

    (B) May contact any other person reasonably believed to be a person at risk of being infected with HIV by that HIV infected person for the purposes of disclosing that such infected person has been determined to be infected with HIV and counseling such person to submit to an HIV test; and

    (C) Shall contact and provide counseling to the spouse of any HIV infected person whose name is thus disclosed if both persons are reasonably likely to have engaged in sexual intercourse or any other act determined by the Department of Public Health likely to have resulted in the transmission of HIV between such persons within the preceding seven years and if that spouse may be located and contacted without undue difficulty.

(h) (h.1) The Department of Public Health may disclose AIDS confidential information regarding a person who has been reported, under paragraph (1) or (2) of subsection (h), to be infected with HIV to a health care provider licensed pursuant to Chapter 11, 26, or 34 of Title 43 whom that person has consulted for medical treatment or advice.

(i) Any health care provider authorized to order an HIV test may disclose AIDS confidential information regarding a patient thereof if that disclosure is made to a health care provider or health care facility which has provided, is providing, or will provide any health care service to that patient and as a result of such provision of service that health care provider or facility:

    (1) Has personnel or patients who may be persons at risk of being infected with HIV by that patient, if that patient is an HIV infected person and such disclosure is reasonably necessary to protect any such personnel or patients from that risk; or

    (2) Has a legitimate need for that information in order to provide that health care service to that patient.

(j) A health care provider or any other person or legal entity authorized but not required to disclose AIDS confidential information pursuant to this Code section shall have no duty to make such disclosure and shall not be liable to the patient or any other person or legal entity for failing to make such disclosure. A health care provider or any other person or legal entity which discloses information as authorized or required by this Code section or as authorized or required by law or rules or regulations made pursuant thereto shall have no civil or criminal liability therefor.

(k) When any person or legal entity is authorized or required by this Code section or any other law to disclose AIDS confidential information to a person at risk of being infected with HIV and that person at risk is a minor or incompetent person, such disclosure may be made to any parent or legal guardian of the minor or incompetent person, to the minor or incompetent person, or to both the minor or incompetent person and any parent or legal guardian thereof.

(l) When an institutional care facility is the site at which a person is at risk of being infected with HIV and as a result of that risk a disclosure of AIDS confidential information to any person at risk at that site is authorized or required under this Code section or any other law, such disclosure may be made to the person at risk or to that institutional care facility's chief administrative or executive officer, or such officer's designee, in which case that officer or designee shall be authorized to make such disclosure to the person at risk.

(m) When a disclosure of AIDS confidential information is authorized or required by this Code section to be made to a physician, health care provider, or legal entity, that disclosure may be made to employees of that physician, health care provider, or legal entity who have been designated thereby to receive such information on behalf thereof. Those designated employees may thereafter disclose to and provide for the disclosure of that information among such other employees of that physician, health care provider, or legal entity, but such disclosures among those employees shall only be authorized when reasonably necessary in the ordinary course of business to carry out the purposes for which that disclosure is authorized or required to be made to that physician, health care provider, or legal entity.

(n) Any disclosure of AIDS confidential information authorized or required by this Code section or any other law and any unauthorized disclosure of such information shall in no way destroy the confidential nature of that information except for the purpose for which the authorized or required disclosure is made.

(o) Any person or legal entity which violates subsection (b) of this Code section shall be guilty of a misdemeanor.

(p) Nothing in this Code section or any other law shall be construed to authorize the disclosure of AIDS confidential information if that disclosure is prohibited by federal law, or regulations promulgated thereunder, nor shall anything in this Code section or any other law be construed to prohibit the disclosure of information which would be AIDS confidential information except that such information does not permit the identification of any person.

(q) A public safety agency or prosecuting attorney may obtain the results from an HIV test to which the person named in the request has submitted under Code Section 15-11-603, 17-10-15, 42-5-52.1, or 42-9-42.1, notwithstanding that the results may be contained in a sealed record.

(r) Any person or legal entity required by an order of a court to disclose AIDS confidential information in the custody or control of such person or legal entity shall disclose that information as required by that order.

(s) AIDS confidential information shall be disclosed as medical information pursuant to Code Section 24-12-1 or pursuant to any other law which authorizes or requires the disclosure of medical information if:

 (1) The person identified by that information:

  (A) Has consented in writing to that disclosure;

  (B) Has been notified of the request for disclosure of that information at least ten days prior to the time the disclosure is to be made and does not object to such disclosure prior to the time specified for that disclosure in that notice; or

  (C) Is suspected of being mentally ill and is the subject of an order issued pursuant to Code Section 37-3-41 when the court issuing such order finds in an in camera hearing by clear and convincing evidence a compelling need for the information which cannot be accommodated by other means. In assessing compelling need, the court shall weigh the public health, safety, or welfare needs or any other public or private need for the disclosure against the privacy interest of the person identified by the information and the public interest which may be disserved by disclosures which may deter voluntary HIV tests. If the court determines that disclosure of that information is authorized under this subparagraph, the court shall order that disclosure and impose appropriate safeguards against any unauthorized disclosure. The records of that hearing otherwise shall be under seal; or

 (2) A superior court in an in camera hearing finds by clear and convincing evidence a compelling need for the information which cannot be accommodated by other means. In assessing compelling need, the court shall weigh the public health, safety, or welfare needs or any other public or private need for the disclosure against the privacy interest of the person identified by the information and the public interest which may be disserved by disclosures which may deter voluntary HIV tests. If the court determines that disclosure of that information is authorized under this paragraph, the court shall order that disclosure and impose appropriate safeguards against any unauthorized disclosure. The records of that hearing otherwise shall be under seal.

(t)

 (1) A superior court of this state may order a person or legal entity to disclose AIDS confidential information in its custody or control to:

  (A) A prosecutor in connection with a prosecution for the alleged commission of reckless conduct under subsection (c) of Code Section 16-5-60;

  (B) Any party in a civil proceeding; or

  (C) A public safety agency or the Department of Public Health if that agency or department has an employee thereof who has, in the course of that employment, come in contact with the body fluids of the person identified by the AIDS confidential information sought in such a manner reasonably likely to cause that employee to become an HIV infected person and provided the disclosure is necessary for the health and safety of that employee,

and, for purposes of this subsection, the term "petitioner for disclosure" means any person or legal entity specified in subparagraph (A), (B), or (C) of this paragraph.

(2) An order may be issued against a person or legal entity responsible for recording, reporting, or maintaining AIDS confidential information to compel the disclosure of that information if the petitioner for disclosure demonstrates by clear and convincing evidence a compelling need for the information which cannot be accommodated by other means. In assessing compelling need, the court shall weigh the public health, safety, or welfare needs or any other public or private need for the disclosure against the privacy interest of the person identified by the information and the public interest which may be disserved by disclosures which may deter voluntary HIV tests.

(3) A petition seeking disclosure of AIDS confidential information under this subsection shall substitute a pseudonym for the true name of the person concerning whom the information is sought. The disclosure to the parties of that person's true name shall be communicated confidentially, in documents not filed with the court.

(4) Before granting any order under this subsection, the court shall provide the person concerning whom the information is sought with notice and a reasonable opportunity to participate in the proceedings if that person is not already a party.

(5) Court proceedings as to disclosure of AIDS confidential information under this subsection shall be conducted in camera unless the person concerning whom the information is sought agrees to a hearing in open court.

(6) Upon the issuance of an order that a person or legal entity be required to disclose AIDS confidential information regarding a person named in that order, that person or entity so ordered shall disclose to the ordering court any such information which is in the control or custody of that person or entity and which relates to the person named in the order for the court to make an in camera inspection thereof. If the court determines from that inspection that the person named in the order is an HIV infected person, the court shall disclose to the petitioner for disclosure that determination and shall impose appropriate safeguards against unauthorized disclosure which shall specify the persons who may have access to the information, the purposes for which the information shall be used, and appropriate prohibitions on future disclosure.

(7) The record of the proceedings under this subsection shall be sealed by the court.

(8) An order may not be issued under this subsection against the Department of Public Health, any county board of health, or any anonymous HIV test site operated by or on behalf of that department.

(u) A health care provider, health care facility, or other person or legal entity who, in violation of this Code section, unintentionally discloses AIDS confidential information, notwithstanding the maintenance of procedures thereby which are reasonably adopted to avoid risk of such disclosure, shall not be civilly or criminally liable, unless such disclosure was due to gross negligence or wanton and willful misconduct.

(v) AIDS confidential information may be disclosed when that disclosure is otherwise authorized or required by Code Section 42-1-6, if AIDS or HIV infection is the communicable disease at issue, or when that disclosure is otherwise authorized or required by any law which specifically refers to "AIDS confidential information," "HIV test results," or any similar language indicating a legislative intent to disclose information specifically relating to AIDS or HIV.

(w) A health care provider who has received AIDS confidential information regarding a patient from the patient's health care provider directly or indirectly under the provisions of subsection (i) of this Code section may disclose that information to a health care provider which has provided, is providing, or will provide any health care service to that patient and as a result of that provision of service that health care provider:

    (1) Has personnel or patients who may be persons at risk of being infected with HIV by that patient, if that patient is an HIV infected person and such disclosure is reasonably necessary to protect any such personnel or patients from that risk; or

    (2) Has a legitimate need for that information in order to provide that health care service to that patient.

(x) Neither the Department of Public Health nor any county board of health shall disclose AIDS confidential information contained in its records unless such disclosure is authorized or required by this Code section or any other law, except that such information in those records shall not be a public record and shall not be subject to disclosure through subpoena, court order, or other judicial process.

(y) The protection against disclosure provided by Code Section 24-12-20 shall be waived and AIDS confidential information may be disclosed to the extent that the person identified by such information, his or her heirs, successors, assigns, or a beneficiary of such person, including, but not limited to, an executor, administrator, or personal representative of such person's estate:

    (1) Files a claim or claims other entitlements under any insurance policy or benefit plan or is involved in any civil proceeding regarding such claim;

    (2) Places such person's care and treatment, the nature and extent of his or her injuries, the extent of his or her damages, his or her medical

condition, or the reasons for his or her death at issue in any judicial proceeding; or

(3) Is involved in a dispute regarding coverage under any insurance policy or benefit plan.

(z) AIDS confidential information may be collected, used, and disclosed by an insurer in accordance with the provisions of Chapter 39 of Title 33.

(aa) In connection with any judicial proceeding in which AIDS confidential information is disclosed as authorized or required by this Code section, the party to whom that information is thereby disclosed may subpoena any person to authenticate such AIDS confidential information, establish a chain of custody relating thereto, or otherwise testify regarding that information, including, but not limited to, testifying regarding any notifications to the patient regarding results of an HIV test. The provisions of this subsection shall apply to records, personnel, or both of the Department of Public Health or a county board of health notwithstanding Code Section 50-18-72, but only as to test results obtained by a prosecutor under subsection (q) of this Code section and to be used thereby in a prosecution for reckless conduct under subsection (c) of Code Section 16-5-60.

(bb) AIDS confidential information may be disclosed as a part of any proceeding or procedure authorized or required pursuant to Chapter 3, 4, or 7 of Title 37, regarding a person who is alleged to be or who is mentally ill, developmentally disabled, or alcoholic or drug dependent, or as a part of any proceeding or procedure authorized or required pursuant to Title 29, regarding the guardianship of a person or that person's estate, as follows:

(1) Any person who files or transmits a petition or other document which discloses AIDS confidential information in connection with any such proceeding or procedure shall provide a cover page which contains only the type of proceeding or procedure, the court in which the proceeding or procedure is or will be pending, and the words "CONFIDENTIAL INFORMATION" without in any way otherwise disclosing thereon the name of any individual or that such petition or other document specifically contains AIDS confidential information;

(2) AIDS confidential information shall only be disclosed pursuant to this subsection after disclosure to and with the written consent of the person identified by that information, or that person's parent or guardian if that person is a minor or has previously been adjudicated as being incompetent, or by order of court obtained in accordance with subparagraph (C) of paragraph (3) of this subsection;

(3) If any person files or transmits a petition or other document in connection with any such proceeding or procedure which discloses AIDS confidential information without obtaining consent as provided in paragraph (2) of this subsection, the court receiving such information shall either obtain written consent as set forth in that paragraph (2) for any further use or disclosure of such information or:

(A) Return such petition or other document to the person who filed or transmitted same, with directions against further filing or transmittal of such information in connection with such proceeding or procedure except in compliance with this subsection;

(B) Delete or expunge all references to such AIDS confidential information from the particular petition or other document; or

(C)

    (i) If the court determines there is a compelling need for such information in connection with the particular proceeding or procedure, petition a superior court of competent jurisdiction for permission to obtain or disclose that information. If the person identified by the information is not yet represented by an attorney in the proceeding or procedure in connection with which the information is sought, the petitioning court shall appoint an attorney for such person. The petitioning court shall have both that person and that person's attorney personally served with notice of the petition and time and place of the superior court hearing thereon. Such hearing shall not be held sooner than 72 hours after service, unless the information is to be used in connection with an emergency guardianship proceeding under Code Section 29-4-14, in which event the hearing shall not be held sooner than 48 hours after service.

    (ii) The superior court in which a petition is filed pursuant to division (i) of this subparagraph shall hold an in camera hearing on such petition. The purpose of the hearing shall be to determine whether there is clear and convincing evidence of a compelling need for the AIDS confidential information sought in connection with the particular proceeding or procedure which cannot be accommodated by other means. In assessing compelling need, the superior court shall weigh the public health, safety, or welfare needs or any other public or private need for the disclosure against the privacy interest of the person identified by the information and the public interest which may be disserved by disclosures which may deter voluntary HIV tests. If the court determines that disclosure of that information is authorized under this subparagraph, the court shall order that disclosure and impose appropriate safeguards against any unauthorized disclosure. The records of that hearing otherwise shall be under seal; and

(4) The court having jurisdiction over such proceeding or procedure, when it becomes apparent that AIDS confidential information will likely be or has been disclosed in connection with such proceeding or procedure, shall take such measures as the court determines

appropriate to preserve the confidentiality of the disclosed information to the maximum extent possible. Such measures shall include, without being limited to, closing the proceeding or procedure to the public and sealing all or any part of the records of the proceeding or procedure containing AIDS confidential information. The records of any appeals taken from any such proceeding or procedure shall also be sealed. Furthermore, the court may consult with and obtain the advice of medical experts or other counsel or advisers as to the relevance and materiality of such information in such proceedings or procedures, provided that the identity of the person identified by such information is not thereby revealed.

ARTICLE 4. OTHER CONFIDENTIAL INFORMATION

§ 24-12-30. Confidential nature of certain library records

(a) Circulation and similar records of a library which identify the user of library materials shall not be public records but shall be confidential and shall not be disclosed except:
  (1) To members of the library staff in the ordinary course of business;
  (2) Upon written consent of the user of the library materials or the user's parents or guardian if the user is a minor or ward; or
  (3) Upon appropriate court order or subpoena.
(b) Any disclosure authorized by subsection (a) of this Code section or any unauthorized disclosure of materials made confidential by subsection (a) of this Code section shall not in any way destroy the confidential nature of that material, except for the purpose for which an authorized disclosure is made. A person disclosing material as authorized by subsection (a) of this Code section shall not be liable therefor.

§ 24-12-31. Confidential nature of veterinarian records; disclosure of rabies vaccination record

(a) No veterinarian licensed under Chapter 50 of Title 43 shall be required to disclose any information concerning the veterinarian's care of an animal except on written authorization or other waiver by the veterinarian's client or on appropriate court order or subpoena. Any veterinarian releasing information under written authorization or other waiver by the client or under court order or subpoena shall not be liable to the client or any other person. The confidentiality provided by this Code section shall be waived to the extent that the veterinarian's client places the veterinarian's care and treatment of the animal or the nature and extent of injuries to the animal at issue in any judicial proceeding. As used in this Code section, the term "client" means the owner of the animal or, if the owner of the animal is unknown, the person who presents the animal to the veterinarian for care and treatment.

(b) Notwithstanding the provisions of subsection (a) of this Code section, a veterinarian shall disclose the rabies vaccination history of any animal within such veterinarian's care within 24 hours of receipt of a written request by the physician of any person bitten by such animal.

CHAPTER 13. SECURING ATTENDANCE OF WITNESSES AND PRODUCTION AND PRESERVATION OF EVIDENCE

ARTICLE 1. GENERAL PROVISIONS

§ 24-13-1. Freedom of witnesses from arrest

A witness shall not be arrested on any civil process while attending any court to which he or she is subpoenaed or otherwise required to attend as a witness or while going to or returning from such court. An officer who holds such witness imprisoned after seeing his or her subpoena or being satisfied of the fact that such person was a witness shall be liable for false imprisonment.

§ 24-13-2. Procedure for claiming witness fees

A witness in making a claim or proof of a claim for witness fees for attendance shall indicate the date on which he or she attended and, in the event of a continuance, shall not claim or receive witness fees for any day after the date to which the docket shows the proceeding was continued nor for any day before the continuance was granted on which he or she did not attend.

§ 24-13-3. Witness fee exceptions

(a) A witness shall not receive any witness fees for attendance on a subpoena if such witness is absent from the proceeding, or if the proceeding is continued at any time due to his or her absence, where such absence did not arise from providential cause.
(b) No witness shall receive witness fees from both parties in the same proceeding; the fees of a witness for both parties shall be apportioned equally between the parties unless the costs are all taxed against one party.

§ 24-13-4. Penalty for excessive witness fee claim

A witness who claims more than is due to such witness shall forfeit all witness fees and shall pay to the injured party, in addition thereto, four times the amount so unjustly claimed.

§ 24-13-5. Production of evidence when item not available; oath

When any person is served with a subpoena for the production of evidence or a notice to produce, seeking books in his or her possession to be used as testimony on the trial of any cause, if the person makes oath that he or she cannot produce the books required without suffering a material injury in his or her business and also makes or causes to be made out a full transcript from the books of all the accounts and dealings with the opposite party, has the transcript examined and sworn to by an impartial witness, and produces the same in court, the witness shall be deemed to have complied with the notice to produce or subpoena for the production of evidence.

§ 24-13-6. Procedure when adverse party dissatisfied with response pursuant to Code Section 24-13-5

When the transcript provided for in Code Section 24-13-5 is produced in court, if the adverse party is dissatisfied therewith and swears that he or she believes that the books contain entries material to the adverse party which do not appear in the transcript, the court shall grant him or her a commission directed to certain persons named by the parties and approved by the court. The commission shall cause the person with possession of the books to produce the books required with the person swearing that the books produced are all that he or she has or had that answer to the description in the subpoena or notice to produce. The commission shall examine the books and transmit to the court a full and fair statement of the accounts and entries between the parties under their hand. When received by the court, the statement of the commission shall be deemed a compliance with the notice to produce or subpoena for the production of evidence.

§ 24-13-7. Withdrawal of originals introduced in evidence; substitution of copies; discretion of court

Parties interested and participating in the trial of all cases tried in the courts are authorized and empowered, on the order of the court trying the case, to withdraw from the court and record of the case all original deeds, maps, blueprints, notes, papers, and documents belonging to the parties and which are introduced in evidence on the trial, on substituting therefor, when required by the court, duplicates thereof, verified as such by the parties or their agents, representatives, or attorneys. However, if any such deeds, maps, blueprints, notes, papers, or documents shall be attacked by any party to the case as forgeries, or as not being genuine originals, it shall be in the discretion of the court to require the original deeds, maps, blueprints, notes, papers, or documents so attacked to remain on file in the court as a part of the record in the case.

ARTICLE 2. SUBPOENAS AND NOTICE TO PRODUCE

§ 24-13-20. Applicability

This article shall apply to all civil proceedings and, insofar as consistent with the Constitution, to all criminal proceedings.

§ 24-13-21. Subpoena for attendance of witnesses -- Form; issuance; subpoena in blank

(a) As used in this Code section, the term "subpoena" includes a witness subpoena and a subpoena for the production of evidence.

(b) A subpoena shall state the name of the court, the name of the clerk, and the title of the proceeding and shall command each person to whom it is directed to attend and give testimony or produce evidence at a time and place specified by the subpoena.

(c) The clerk of court shall make subpoenas in blank available on demand by electronic or other means to parties or their counsel or to the grand jury.

(d) An attorney who is counsel of record in a proceeding may issue and sign a subpoena obtained by electronic or other means from the clerk of court as an officer of a court for any deposition, hearing, or trial held in conjunction with such proceeding.

(e) A district attorney may issue, and upon the request of the grand jury shall issue, a subpoena in grand jury proceedings.

(f) A subpoena shall be completed prior to being served.

(g) Subpoenas are enforceable as provided in Code Section 24-13-26.

(h) If an individual misuses a subpoena, he or she shall be subject to punishment for contempt of court and shall be punished by a fine of not more than $300.00 or not more than 20 days' imprisonment, or both.

§ 24-13-22. Subpoena for attendance of witnesses -- Attendance at hearing or trial; where served

At the request of any party, subpoenas for attendance at a hearing or trial shall be issued under the authority of the clerk of the court in which the hearing or trial is held. A subpoena requiring the attendance of a witness at a hearing or trial may be served at any place within this state.

§ 24-13-23. Subpoena for production of documentary evidence; motion to quash or modify

(a) A subpoena may also command the person to whom it is directed to produce the evidence designated therein.

(b) The court, upon written motion made promptly and in any event at or before the time specified in the subpoena for compliance therewith, may:

(1) Quash or modify the subpoena if it is unreasonable and oppressive; or

(2) Condition denial of the motion upon the advancement by the person in whose behalf the subpoena is issued of the reasonable cost of producing the evidence.

§ 24-13-24. Service of subpoenas

A subpoena may be served by any sheriff, by his or her deputy, or by any other person not less than 18 years of age. Proof may be shown by return or certificate endorsed on a copy of the subpoena. Subpoenas may also be served by registered or certified mail or statutory overnight delivery, and the return receipt shall constitute prima-facie proof of service. Service upon a party may be made by serving his or her counsel of record.

§ 24-13-25. Fees and mileage; when tender required

Except as provided in Code Section 24-13-28, the witness fee shall be $25.00 per diem, and execution shall be issued by the clerk upon affidavit of the witness to enforce payment thereof. The payment of witness fees shall not be demanded as a condition precedent to attendance; but, when a witness resides outside the county where the testimony is to be given, service of the subpoena, to be valid, shall be accompanied by tender of the witness fee for one day's attendance plus mileage of 45 cent(s) per mile for traveling expenses for going from and returning to his or her place of residence by the nearest practical route. Tender of witness fees and mileage may be made by United States currency, postal money order, cashier's check, certified check, or the check of an attorney or law firm. When the subpoena is issued on behalf of this state, or an officer, agency, or political subdivision thereof, or an accused in a criminal proceeding, witness fees and mileage need not be tendered.

§ 24-13-26. Enforcement of subpoenas; continuance; secondary evidence of books, papers, or documents

(a) Subpoenas may be enforced by attachment for contempt and by a fine of not more than $300.00 or not more than 20 days' imprisonment, or both. In all proceedings under this Code section, the court shall consider whether under the circumstances of each proceeding the subpoena was served within a reasonable time, but in any event not less than 24 hours prior to the time that appearance thereunder was required.

(b) The court may also in appropriate proceedings grant continuance of the proceeding. Where subpoenas were issued in blank, no continuance shall be granted because of failure to respond thereto when the party obtaining such subpoenas fails to present to the clerk the name and address of the witness so subpoenaed at least six hours before appearance is required.

(c) When evidence is unsuccessfully sought, secondary evidence thereof shall be admissible.

§ 24-13-27. Notice to produce

Where a party desires to compel production of evidence in the possession, custody, or control of another party, in lieu of serving a subpoena under this article, the party desiring the production may serve a notice to produce upon counsel for the other party. Service may be perfected in accordance with Code Section 24-13-24, but no witness fees or mileage shall be allowed therefor. Such notices may be enforced in the manner prescribed by Code Section 24-13-26, and Code Section 24-13-23 shall also apply to such notices. The notice shall be in writing, signed by the party seeking production of the evidence, or the party's attorney, and shall be directed to the opposite party or his or her attorney.

§ 24-13-28. Witness fees for law enforcement officers

(a) As used in this Code section, the term:
    (1) "Director" means the appropriate chief of police, sheriff, director of public safety of a college or university, local fire chief, director of the Georgia Bureau of Investigation, the commanding officer of the Georgia State Patrol, the commissioner of natural resources, the superintendent of a correctional institution, or the state fire marshal.
    (2) "Law enforcement officer" means any member of a municipal or county police force, any deputy sheriff, any campus policeman as defined in Code Section 20-8-1, any member of a local fire department, any member of the Georgia State Patrol or Georgia Bureau of Investigation, any correctional officer, any person employed by the Department of Natural Resources as a law enforcement officer, or any arson investigator of the state fire marshal's office.
    (3) "Regular duty hours" means the daily shift of duty to which a law enforcement officer is assigned and shall not include paid or unpaid vacation, paid or unpaid sick leave, paid or unpaid holiday leave, or any other paid or unpaid leave status established pursuant to the personnel regulations or scheduling practices of the employing agency.

(b) Any law enforcement officer who shall be required by subpoena to attend any superior court, other courts having jurisdiction to enforce the penal laws of this state, municipal court having jurisdiction to enforce the penal laws of this state as provided by Code Section 40-13-21, juvenile court, grand jury, hearing or inquest held or called by a coroner, or magistrate court involving any criminal matter, as a witness on behalf of the state during any hours except the regular duty hours to which the officer is assigned, shall be paid for such attendance at a fixed rate to be established by the governing authority, but not less than $25.00 per diem. The claim for the witness fees shall be endorsed on the subpoena showing the dates of attendance and stating that attendance was required during the hours other than the regular duty hours to which the claimant was assigned. The claimant shall verify this statement. The dates of attendance shall be certified by the judge or the prosecuting attorney of the court attended. The director or his or her designee shall certify that the claimant has not received any overtime pay for his or her attendance and that his or her attendance was required during hours other than regular duty hours. The amount due shall be paid by the governing body authorized to dispense public funds for the operation of the court. However, no such law enforcement officer shall claim or receive more than one witness fee per day for attendance in any court or before the grand jury regardless of the number of subpoenas which the law enforcement officer may have received requiring such officer to appear in such court or before the grand jury on any one day.

(c)

    (1) Except as provided in paragraph (2) of this subsection, any law enforcement officer who shall be required by subpoena to attend any court of this state with respect to any civil proceeding, as a witness concerning any matter relative to the law enforcement duties of such law enforcement officer during any hours except the regular duty hours to which the law enforcement officer is assigned, shall be paid for such attendance at a fixed rate to be established by the governing authority, but not less than $25.00 per diem. Any such law enforcement officer shall also be entitled to the mileage allowance provided in Code Section 24-13-25 when such law enforcement officer resides outside the county where the testimony is to be given. The claim for the witness fees shall be endorsed on the subpoena showing the dates of attendance and stating that attendance was required during the hours other than the regular duty hours to which the claimant was assigned. The claimant shall verify such statement. The dates of attendance shall be certified by the party obtaining the subpoena. The director or his or her designee shall certify that the claimant has not received any overtime pay for the law enforcement officer's attendance and that such law enforcement officer's attendance was required during hours other than regular duty hours.

    (2) Any law enforcement officer covered by paragraph (1) of this subsection who is required by subpoena to attend any court with respect to any civil proceeding, as a witness concerning any matter which is not related to the duties of such law enforcement officer, shall be compensated as provided in Code Section 24-13-25.

(d) The fee specified by subsections (b) and (c) of this Code section shall not be paid if the law enforcement officer receives any overtime pay for time spent attending such court pursuant to the subpoena.

§ 24-13-29. Legislators' exemption

No member of the General Assembly of Georgia shall be compelled to attend and give testimony at any hearing or trial or to produce evidence while the General Assembly is in regular or extraordinary session.

ARTICLE 3. SECURING ATTENDANCE OF PRISONERS

§ 24-13-60. Order requiring prisoner's delivery to serve as witness or criminal defendant generally; expenses; prisoner under death sentence as witness

(a) When a prisoner confined in any state prison, county correctional institution, or other penal institution under the jurisdiction of the Board of Corrections, other than a prisoner under a death sentence, is needed as a witness in any judicial proceeding in any court of record in this state or when it is desired that such person stand trial on an indictment or accusation charging the prisoner with commission of a felony or misdemeanor, the judge of the court wherein the proceeding is pending shall be authorized to and shall issue an ex parte order, directed to the commissioner of corrections, requiring the prisoner's delivery to the sheriff of the county where the prisoner is desired as a witness or accused. The sheriff or his or her deputies shall take custody of the prisoner on the date named in the order, safely keep the prisoner pending the proceeding, and return him or her to the original place of detention after the prisoner's discharge by the trial judge.

(b) If the prisoner was desired as a witness by this state in a criminal proceeding or if the prisoner's release to the sheriff was for the purpose of standing trial on criminal charges, the county wherein the proceeding was pending shall pay all expenses of transportation and keeping, including per diem and mileage of the sheriff, jail fees, and any other proper expense approved by the trial judge.

(c) If the prisoner was desired as a witness by the accused in a criminal proceeding or by either party to a civil proceeding, the costs and expenses referred to in subsection (b) of this Code section shall be borne by the party requesting the prisoner as a witness. The court shall require a deposit of money sufficient to defray same, except where the judge, after examining into the matter, determines that the prisoner's presence is required by the interests of justice and that the party requesting it is financially unable to make the deposit, in which case the expenses shall be taxed as costs of court.

(d) If a prisoner under a death sentence is needed as a witness for either the prosecution or the defense in any felony case, the requesting party may interview the proposed witness. Following such interview, the requesting party may move for a writ of habeas corpus ad testificandum. Such motion shall be accompanied by a proffer of the testimony of the proposed witness. The requesting party shall make such motion and proffer as soon as possible but shall not make such motion later than 20 days prior to the date of the trial. Nothing in this Code section shall limit the right of a party from presenting a material witness at a hearing or trial and to have compulsory process for that purpose.

§ 24-13-61. Issuance of order requiring prisoner's delivery to serve as witness in superior court

Any judge of the superior court may issue an order to any officer having a lawfully imprisoned person in his or her custody, requiring the production of such person before the court for the purpose of giving evidence in any criminal cause pending therein, without any formal application or writ of habeas corpus ad testificandum for that purpose.

§ 24-13-62. Issuance of writ of habeas corpus requiring prisoner's delivery to serve as witness in superior court

The writ of habeas corpus ad testificandum may be issued by the superior court to cause the production in court of any witness under legal imprisonment.

ARTICLE 4. UNIFORM ACT TO SECURE THE ATTENDANCE OF WITNESSES FROM WITHOUT THE STATE

§ 24-13-90. Short title

This article shall be known and may be cited as "The Uniform Act to Secure the Attendance of Witnesses from Without the State."

§ 24-13-91. Definitions

As used in this article, the term:
   (1) "Penal institution" means a jail, prison, penitentiary, house of correction, or other place of penal detention.
   (2) "State" means any state or territory of the United States and the District of Columbia.
   (3) "Summons" means a subpoena, order, or other notice requiring the appearance of a witness.
   (4) "Witness" means a person whose testimony is desired in any proceeding or investigation by a grand jury or in a criminal prosecution or proceeding held by the prosecution or the defense, including a person who is confined in a penal institution in any state.

§ 24-13-92. Criminal or grand jury proceeding in foreign state -- Certificate of need for testimony; expenses; punishment

(a) If a judge of a court of record in any state which by its laws has made provision for commanding persons within that state to attend and testify in this state certifies under the seal of such court that there is a criminal prosecution pending in such court or that a grand jury investigation has commenced or is about to commence, that a person within this state is a material witness in such prosecution or grand jury investigation, and that the witness's presence will be required for a specified number of days, upon presentation of such certificate to any judge of a court of record in the county in which the person is found, such judge shall fix a time and place for a hearing and shall make an order directing the witness to appear at a time and place certain for the hearing. The witness shall at all times be entitled to counsel.

(b) If at a hearing the judge determines that the witness is material and necessary, that it will not cause undue hardship to the witness to be compelled to attend and testify in the prosecution or a grand jury investigation in the other state, and the laws of the state in which the prosecution is pending or grand jury investigation has commenced or is about to commence will give to such witness protection from arrest and the service of civil and criminal process, the judge shall issue a summons, with a copy of the certificate attached, directing the witness to attend and testify in the court where the prosecution is pending or where a grand jury investigation has commenced or is about to commence at a time and place specified in the summons. In any such hearing, the certificate shall be prima-facie evidence of all the facts stated therein.

(c) If such certificate recommends that the witness be taken into immediate custody and delivered to an officer of the requesting state to assure the witness's attendance in the requesting state, such judge may, in lieu of notification of the hearing, direct that the witness be forthwith brought before him or her for the hearing; and the judge at the hearing being satisfied of the desirability of such custody and delivery, for which determination the certificate shall be prima-facie proof of such desirability, may, in lieu of issuing a subpoena or summons, order that the witness be forthwith taken into custody and delivered to an officer of the requesting state.

(d) If the witness, who is summoned as above provided, after being paid or tendered by some properly authorized person the sum of 45 cent(s) a mile for each mile by the ordinarily traveled route to and from the court where the prosecution is pending and $25.00 for each day that the witness is required to travel and attend as a witness, fails without good cause to attend and testify as directed in the summons, the witness shall be punished in the manner provided for in Code Section 24-13-26.

§ 24-13-93. Criminal or grand jury proceeding in foreign state -- Certificate of need for prisoner's testimony; order by judge in requesting state; applicability

(a) A judge of a state court of record in another state which by its laws has made provision for commanding persons confined in penal institutions within that state to attend and testify in this state may certify that there is a criminal proceeding or investigation by a grand jury or a criminal proceeding pending in the court, that a person who is confined in a penal institution in this state is a material witness in the proceeding or investigation, and that the witness's presence will be required during a specified time. Upon presentation of the certificate to any judge having jurisdiction over the person confined and upon notice to the Attorney General, the judge in this state shall fix a time and place for a hearing and shall make an order directed to the person having custody of the prisoner requiring that the prisoner be produced before him or her at the hearing.

(b) If at the hearing the judge determines that the witness is material and necessary, that the witness attending and testifying are not adverse to the interest of this state or to the health and legal rights of the witness, that the laws of the state in which the witness is required to testify will give the witness protection from arrest and the service of civil and criminal process because of any act committed prior to the witness's arrival in the state under the order, and that as a practical matter the possibility is negligible that the witness may be subject to arrest or to the service of civil or criminal process in any state through which the witness will be required to pass, the judge shall issue an order, with a copy of the certificate attached, directing the witness to attend and testify, directing the person having custody of the witness to produce the witness in the court where the criminal proceeding is pending or where the grand jury investigation is pending at a time and place specified in the order, and prescribing such conditions as the judge shall determine. The judge, in lieu of directing the person having custody of the witness to produce the witness in the requesting jurisdiction's court, may direct and require in the court's order that the requesting jurisdiction shall come to the Georgia penal institution in which the witness is confined to accept custody of the witness for physical transfer to the requesting jurisdiction; that the requesting jurisdiction shall provide proper safeguards on the witness's custody while in transit; that the requesting jurisdiction shall be liable for and shall pay all expenses incurred in producing and returning the witness, including, but not limited to, food, lodging, clothing, and medical care; and that the requesting jurisdiction shall promptly deliver the witness back to the same or another Georgia penal institution as specified by the Department of Corrections at the conclusion of his or her testimony.

(c) The order to the witness and to the person having custody of the witness shall provide for the return of the witness at the conclusion of his or her testimony, proper safeguards on his or her custody, and proper financial reimbursement or prepayment by the requesting jurisdiction of all expenses incurred in the production and return of the witness and may prescribe such other conditions as the judge thinks proper or necessary. If the judge directs and requires the requesting jurisdiction to accept custody of the witness at the Georgia penal institution in which the witness is confined and to deliver the witness back to the same or another Georgia penal institution at the conclusion of the witness's testimony, no prepayment of expenses shall be necessary. The order shall not become effective until the judge of the state requesting the witness enters an order directing compliance with the conditions prescribed.

(d) This Code section shall not apply to any person in this state confined as insane or mentally ill or under sentence of death.

§ 24-13-94. Criminal or grand jury proceeding in this state -- Issuance of certificate; how long witness detained; punishment

(a) If a person in any state which by its laws has made provision for commanding persons within its borders to attend and testify in criminal prosecutions or grand jury investigations commenced or about to commence in this state is a material witness in a prosecution pending in a court of record in this state or in a grand jury investigation which has commenced or is about to commence a judge of such court may issue a certificate under the seal of the court stating these facts and specifying the number of days the witness will be required. The certificate may include a recommendation that the witness be taken into immediate custody and delivered to an officer of this state to assure attendance in this state. This certificate shall be presented to a judge of a court of record in the county in which the witness is found.

(b) If the witness is summoned to attend and testify in this state, the witness shall be tendered the sum of 45 cent(s) a mile for each mile by the ordinarily traveled route to and from the court where the prosecution is pending and $25.00 for each day that the witness is required to travel and attend as a witness. A witness who has appeared in accordance with the provisions of the summons shall not be required to remain within this state for a longer period of time than the period mentioned in the certificate, unless otherwise ordered by the court. If such witness, after coming into this state, fails without good cause to attend and testify as directed in the summons, the witness shall be punished in the manner provided for in Code Section 24-13-26.

§ 24-13-95. Criminal or grand jury proceeding in this state -- Issuance of certificate seeking testimony of prisoner; notice to attorney general; order of compliance

(a) If a person confined in a penal institution in any other state is a material witness in a criminal proceeding pending in a court of record or in a grand jury investigation in this state, a judge of the court may certify that there is a criminal proceeding or investigation by a grand jury or a criminal proceeding pending in the court, that a person who is confined in a penal institution in the other state is a material witness in the proceeding or investigation, and that the witness's presence will be required during a specified time. The certificate shall be presented to a judge of a court of record in the other state having jurisdiction over the confined prisoner, and a notice shall be given to the attorney general of the state in which the prisoner is confined.

(b) The judge of the court in this state may enter an order directing compliance with the terms and conditions prescribed by the judge of the state in which the witness is confined.

§ 24-13-96. Exemption of witnesses from arrest and service of process

(a) If a person comes into this state in obedience to a summons directing him or her to attend and testify in this state, such person shall not while in this state pursuant to such summons be subject to arrest or the service of process, civil or criminal, in connection with matters which arose before such person's entrance into this state under the summons.

(b) If a person passes through this state while going to another state in obedience to a summons to attend and testify in that state or while returning therefrom, he or she shall not while so passing through this state be subject to arrest or the service of process, civil or criminal, in connection with matters which arose before such person's entrance into this state under the summons.

§ 24-13-97. Construction

This article shall be interpreted and construed so as to effectuate its general purpose to make uniform the laws of the states which enact it and shall be applicable only to such states as shall enact reciprocal powers to this state relative to the matter of securing attendance of witnesses as provided in this article.

ARTICLE 5. UNIFORM INTERSTATE DEPOSITIONS AND DISCOVERY ACT

§ 24-13-110. Short title

This article shall be known and may be cited as the "Uniform Interstate Depositions and Discovery Act."

§ 24-13-111. Definitions

As used in this article, the term:
  (1) "Foreign jurisdiction" means a state other than this state.
  (2) "Foreign subpoena" means a subpoena issued under authority of a court of record of a foreign jurisdiction.
  (3) "Person" means an individual, corporation, business trust, estate, trust, partnership, limited liability company, association, joint venture, public corporation, government or governmental subdivision, agency, or instrumentality, or any other legal or commercial entity.
  (4) "State" means a state of the United States, the District of Columbia, Puerto Rico, the United States Virgin Islands, a federally recognized

Native American tribe, or any territory or insular possession subject to the jurisdiction of the United States.

(5) "Subpoena" means a document, however denominated, issued under authority of a court of record requiring a person to:

(A) Attend and give testimony at a deposition;

(B) Produce and permit inspection and copying of designated books, documents, records, electronically stored information, or tangible things in the possession, custody, or control of such person; or

(C) Permit inspection of premises under the control of such person.

§ 24-13-112. Requirements for issuance of foreign subpoenas; application

(a) To request issuance of a subpoena under this Code section, a party shall submit a foreign subpoena to the clerk of superior court of the county in which the person receiving the subpoena resides. A request for the issuance of a subpoena under this Code section shall not constitute an appearance in the courts of this state.

(b) When a party submits a foreign subpoena to a clerk of superior court in this state, the clerk shall promptly issue and provide to the requestor a subpoena for service upon the person to which the foreign subpoena is directed.

(c) A subpoena under subsection (b) of this Code section shall:

(1) Incorporate the terms used in the foreign subpoena; and

(2) Contain or be accompanied by the names, addresses, and telephone numbers of all counsel of record in the proceeding to which the subpoena relates and of any party not represented by counsel.

(d) This Code section shall only apply to a subpoena to be issued in this state if the foreign jurisdiction that issued the foreign subpoena has adopted a version of the "Uniform Interstate Depositions and Discovery Act."

(e) This Code section shall not apply to criminal proceedings.

§ 24-13-113. Compelling foreign witness to appear and testify

(a) For purposes of this Code section, the term "subpoena" shall have only the meaning set forth in subparagraph (A) of paragraph (5) of Code Section 24-13-111.

(b) In addition to the mechanism for issuing subpoenas provided for in Code Section 24-13-112, whenever any mandate, writ, or commission is issued out of any court of record in a foreign jurisdiction, a witness may be compelled by subpoena issued by the clerk of superior court of the county in which such witness resides to appear and testify in the same manner and by the same process and proceeding as may be employed for the purpose of taking testimony in proceedings pending in this state.

§ 24-13-114. Service of foreign subpoena

A subpoena issued by the clerk of superior court under Code Section 24-13-112 or 24-13-113 shall be served in compliance with Code Section 24-13-23 and shall be served within a reasonable time prior to the appearance required by such subpoena.

§ 24-13-115. Applicability of Article 2 to certain provisions of this article

Article 2 of this chapter shall apply to subpoenas issued under Code Section 24-13-112 or 24-13-113.

§ 24-13-116. Protective order or enforcement, quashing, or modification of foreign subpoena

An application for a protective order or to enforce, quash, or modify a subpoena issued by the clerk of superior court under Code Section 24-13-112 or 24-13-113 shall comply with the statutes and court rules of this state and shall be submitted to the superior court of the county in which the subpoena was issued.

ARTICLE 6. DEPOSITIONS TO PRESERVE TESTIMONY IN CRIMINAL PROCEEDINGS

§ 24-13-130. When deposition to preserve testimony in criminal proceedings may be taken

(a)

 (1) At any time after an accused has been charged with an offense against the laws of this state or an ordinance of any political subdivision or authority thereof, upon motion of the state or the accused, the court having jurisdiction to try the offense charged may, after notice to the parties, order that the testimony of a prospective material witness of a party be taken by deposition and that any designated evidence not privileged be produced at the same time and place.

 (2) At any time after an accused has been charged with an offense of child molestation, aggravated child molestation, or physical or sexual abuse of a child, upon motion of the state or the accused, the court having jurisdiction to try the offense charged may, after notice to the parties, order that the testimony of any physician whose testimony is relevant to such charge be taken by deposition and that any designated evidence not privileged be produced at the same time and place.

(b) The court shall not order the taking of the witness's testimony, except as provided in paragraph (2) of subsection (a) of this Code section, unless it appears to the satisfaction of the court that the testimony of the witness is material to the proceeding and the witness:

(1) Is in imminent danger of death or great bodily harm;

(2) Has been threatened with death or great bodily harm because of the witness's status as a potential witness in a criminal trial or proceeding;

(3) Is about to leave this state, and there are reasonable grounds to believe that such witness will be unable to attend a criminal trial or proceeding;

(4) Is so sick or infirm as to afford reasonable grounds to believe that such witness will be unable to testify as a witness at a criminal trial or proceeding;

(5) Is being detained as a material witness, and there are reasonable grounds to believe that the witness will flee if released from detention; or

(6) Is 72 years of age or older.

(c) A motion to take a deposition of a material witness, or a physician as provided in paragraph (2) of subsection (a) of this Code section, shall be verified and shall state:

(1) The nature of the offense charged;

(2) The status of the criminal proceedings;

(3) The name of the witness and an address in Georgia where the witness may be contacted unless, for good cause shown, the court allows an exception to this paragraph;

(4) That the testimony of the witness is material to the proceeding or that the witness is a physician as provided in paragraph (2) of subsection (a) of this Code section; and

(5) The basis for taking the deposition as provided in subsection (b) of this Code section.

(d) A motion to take a deposition shall be filed in the court having jurisdiction to try the accused for the offense charged; provided, however, that if the accused is charged with multiple offenses, only the court having jurisdiction to try the most serious charge against the accused shall have jurisdiction to hear and decide the motion to take a deposition.

(e) The party moving the court for an order pursuant to this Code section shall give not less than one day's notice of the hearing to the opposite party. A copy of the motion shall be sent to the opposing party or his or her counsel by any means which will reasonably ensure timely delivery, including transmission by facsimile or by digital or electronic means. A copy of the notice shall be attached to the motion and filed with the clerk of court.

(f) If the court is satisfied that the examination of the witness is authorized by law and necessary, the court shall enter an order setting a time period of not more than 30 days during which the deposition shall be taken.

(g) On motion of either party, the court may designate a judge who shall be available to rule on any objections to the interrogation of the witness or before whom the deposition shall be taken. The judge so designated may be a judge of any court of this state who is otherwise qualified to preside over the trial of criminal proceedings in the court having jurisdiction over the offense charged.

§ 24-13-131. Notice of deposition; presence of defendant at examination; child witness

(a) The party at whose instance a deposition is to be taken shall give to every party reasonable written notice of the time and place for taking the deposition. The notice shall state the name and address of each person to be examined.

(b) On motion of a party upon whom the notice is served, the court for cause shown may extend or shorten the time or change the place for taking the deposition.

(c) The officer having custody of an accused shall be notified of the time and place set for the examination and shall, unless the accused waives in writing the right to be present, produce the accused at the examination and keep the accused in the presence of the witness during the examination unless, after being warned by the judge that disruptive conduct will cause the accused's removal from the place where the deposition is being taken, the accused persists in conduct which would justify exclusion from that place.

(d) An accused not in custody shall have the right to be present at the examination; but failure of the accused to appear, absent good cause shown, after notice and tender of expenses, shall constitute a waiver of that right and of any objection to the taking and use of the deposition based upon that right.

(e) Notwithstanding the provisions of subsections (c) and (d) of this Code section, if the witness is a child, the court may order that the deposition be taken in accordance with Code Section 17-8-55.

§ 24-13-132. Appointment of counsel; payment of costs and expenses

(a) If an accused is financially unable to employ counsel, the court shall appoint counsel as provided in Chapter 12 of Title 17, unless the accused elects to proceed without counsel.

(b) Whenever a deposition is taken at the instance of the state, the cost of any such deposition shall be paid by the state by the Prosecuting Attorneys' Council of the State of Georgia out of such funds as may be appropriated for the operations of the district attorneys.

(c) Depositions taken at the instance of an accused shall be paid for by the accused; provided, however, that, whenever a deposition is taken at the instance of an accused who is eligible for the appointment of counsel as provided in Chapter 12 of Title 17, the court shall direct that the reasonable expenses for the taking of the deposition and of travel and subsistence of the accused and the accused's attorney for attendance at the examination, not to exceed the limits established pursuant to Article 2 of

Chapter 7 of Title 45, be paid for out of the fine and bond forfeiture fund of the county where venue is laid.

§ 24-13-133. Manner of taking and filing deposition

Except as provided in Code Section 24-13-137, a deposition shall be taken and filed in the manner provided in civil proceedings, provided that (1) in no event shall a deposition be taken of an accused party without his or her consent and (2) the scope of examination and cross-examination shall be such as would be allowed in the trial itself. On request or waiver by the accused, the court may direct that a deposition be taken on written interrogatories in the manner provided in civil proceedings. Such request shall constitute a waiver by the accused of any objection to the taking and use of the deposition based upon its being so taken. If a judge has been designated to rule on objections or to preside over the deposition, objections to interrogation of the witness shall be made to and ruled on by such judge in the same manner as at the trial of a criminal proceeding.

§ 24-13-134. Availability to state and defendant of deponent's previous statements

The state or the accused shall make available to each other, for examination and use at the taking of a deposition pursuant to this article, any statement of the witness being deposed which is in the possession of the state or the accused and which would be required to be made available if the witness were testifying at the trial.

§ 24-13-135. Admissibility and use of deposition

At the trial or upon any hearing, a part or all of a deposition, so far as otherwise admissible under the rules of evidence, may be used if the witness is unavailable. Any deposition may also be used by any party for the purpose of contradicting or impeaching the testimony of the deponent as a witness. If only a part of a deposition is offered in evidence by a party, an adverse party may require the offering of all of it which is relevant to the part offered, and any party may offer other parts. A witness is not unavailable if the exemption, refusal to testify, claim of lack of memory, inability, or absence of such witness is due to the procurement or wrongdoing of the party offering the deposition at the hearing or trial for the purpose of preventing the witness from attending or testifying.

§ 24-13-136. Objections to admission of deposition

Objections to receiving in evidence a deposition or part thereof may be made as provided in civil proceedings.

§ 24-13-137. Recordation of deposition

(a) Any party shall have the right to require that the deposition be recorded and preserved by the use of audio-visual equipment in addition to a stenographic record. The audio-visual recording shall be transmitted to the clerk of the court which ordered the deposition and shall be made available for viewing and copying only to the prosecuting attorney and accused's attorney prior to trial. An audio-visual recording made pursuant to this Code section shall not be available for inspection or copying by the public until such audio-visual recording has been admitted into evidence during a trial or hearing in the case in which such deposition is made.

(b) An audio-visual recording made pursuant to this Code section may be admissible at a trial or hearing as an alternative to the stenographic record of the deposition.

(c) A stenographic record of the deposition contemplated in this Code section shall be made pursuant to Code Section 9-11-28.

§ 24-13-138. Agreement of parties to deposition

Nothing in this article shall preclude the taking of a deposition, orally or upon written questions, or the use of a deposition by agreement of the parties with the consent of the court.

§ 24-13-139. Depositions taken only in exceptional circumstances; misuse of procedures

It is the intent of the General Assembly that depositions shall be taken in criminal proceedings only in exceptional circumstances when it is in the interests of justice that the testimony of a prospective witness be taken and preserved for use at trial. If the court finds that any party or counsel for a party is using the procedures set forth in this article for the purpose of harassment or delay, such conduct may be punished as contempt of court.

ARTICLE 7. PERPETUATION OF TESTIMONY

§ 24-13-150. When proceedings to perpetuate testimony may be had

Superior courts may entertain proceedings for the perpetuation of testimony in all proceedings in which the fact to which the testimony relates cannot immediately be made the subject of investigation at law and in which, for any cause, the common-law proceeding authorized under this title is not as available, or as completely available, as a proceeding in equity.

§ 24-13-151. Inadequacy of usual proceeding to be shown

A petition for discovery merely or to perpetuate testimony shall not be sustained unless some reason is shown why the usual proceeding at law is inadequate.

§ 24-13-152. Materiality of possession of property; of availability of parties in interest

The possession of the property is immaterial; nor shall the proceeding be denied though all parties in interest cannot be ascertained or reached.

§ 24-13-153. Use of testimony

Testimony taken in the proceedings contemplated under Code Section 24-13-150 shall be used only from the necessity of the case, but in such case may be used against all persons, whether parties to the proceeding or not.

§ 24-13-154. Costs of proceedings

The complainant shall in all cases be taxed with the costs of proceedings to perpetuate testimony.

CHAPTER 14. PROOF GENERALLY

ARTICLE 1. GENERAL PROVISIONS

§ 24-14-1. On whom burden of proof lies

The burden of proof generally lies upon the party who is asserting or affirming a fact and to the existence of whose case or defense the proof of such fact is essential. If a negation or negative affirmation is essential to a party's case or defense, the proof of such negation or negative affirmation shall lie on the party so affirming it.

§ 24-14-2. Change of burden in discretion of court

What amount of evidence will change the onus or burden of proof shall be a question to be decided in each case by the sound discretion of the court.

§ 24-14-3. Amount of mental conviction required; preponderance of evidence in civil cases

Moral and reasonable certainty is all that can be expected in legal investigation. Except as provided in Code Section 51-1-29.5 or Code Section 51-12-5.1, in all civil proceedings, a preponderance of evidence shall be considered sufficient to produce mental conviction. In criminal proceedings, a greater strength of mental conviction shall be held necessary to justify a verdict of guilty.

§ 24-14-4. Determining where preponderance of evidence lies

In determining where the preponderance of evidence lies, the jury may consider all the facts and circumstances of the case, the witnesses' manner of testifying, their intelligence, their means and opportunity for knowing the facts to which they testified, the nature of the facts to which they testified, the probability or improbability of their testimony, their interest or want of interest, and their personal credibility so far as the same may legitimately appear from the trial. The jury may also consider the number of the witnesses, though the preponderance is not necessarily with the greater number.

§ 24-14-5. Reasonable doubt in criminal cases

Whether dependent upon direct or circumstantial evidence, the true question in criminal cases is not whether it is possible that the conclusion at which the evidence points may be false, but whether there is sufficient evidence to satisfy the mind and conscience beyond a reasonable doubt.

§ 24-14-6. When conviction may be had on circumstantial evidence

To warrant a conviction on circumstantial evidence, the proved facts shall not only be consistent with the hypothesis of guilt, but shall exclude every other reasonable hypothesis save that of the guilt of the accused.

§ 24-14-7. Positive testimony preferred over negative; exception

The existence of a fact testified to by one positive witness is to be believed, rather than that such fact did not exist because many other witnesses who had the same opportunity of observation swear that they did not see or know of its having existed. This rule shall not apply when two parties have equal facilities for seeing or hearing a thing and one swears that it occurred while the other swears that it did not.

§ 24-14-8. Number of witnesses required generally; exceptions; effect of corroboration

The testimony of a single witness is generally sufficient to establish a fact. However, in certain cases, including prosecutions for treason, prosecutions for perjury, and felony cases where the only witness is an accomplice, the testimony of a single witness shall not be sufficient. Nevertheless, corroborating circumstances may dispense with the necessity for the testimony of a second witness, except in prosecutions for treason.

§ 24-14-9. Inferences from evidence or lack thereof

In arriving at a verdict, the jury, from facts proved, and sometimes from the absence of counter evidence, may infer the existence of other facts reasonably and logically consequent on those proved.

ARTICLE 2. PRESUMPTIONS AND ESTOPPEL

§ 24-14-20. Presumptions of law and of fact distinguished

Presumptions are either of law or of fact. Presumptions of law are conclusions and inferences which the law draws from given facts. Presumptions of fact shall be exclusively questions for the jury, to be decided by the ordinary test of human experience.

§ 24-14-21. Rebuttable presumptions of law

Certain presumptions of law, such as the presumption of innocence, in some cases the presumption of guilt, the presumption of continuance of life for seven years, the presumption of a mental state once proved to exist, and all similar presumptions, may be rebutted by proof.

§ 24-14-22. Presumption from failure to produce evidence

If a party has evidence in such party's power and within such party's reach by which he or she may repel a claim or charge against him or her but omits to produce it or if such party has more certain and satisfactory evidence in his or her power but relies on that which is of a weaker and inferior nature, a presumption arises that the charge or claim against such party is well founded; but this presumption may be rebutted.

§ 24-14-23. Presumption from failure to answer business letter

In the ordinary course of business, when good faith requires an answer, it is the duty of the party receiving a letter from another to answer within a reasonable time. Otherwise, the party shall be presumed to admit the propriety of the acts mentioned in the letter of the party's correspondent and to adopt them.

§ 24-14-24. Presumption of occupancy of railroad right of way

In any proceeding to establish a right, title, or interest in or to real property that is a part of a railroad right of way, including a right of ingress or egress, where such proceeding is based upon occupancy of the railroad right of way by a person or entity other than the railroad corporation or railroad company, there shall be a presumption that any such occupancy of the railroad right of way is with the permission of the railroad corporation or railroad company. Such presumption may be rebutted.

§ 24-14-25. Presumption of payment of check

(a) As used in this Code section:

(1) "Bank" means any person engaged in the business of banking and includes, in addition to a commercial bank, a savings and loan association, savings bank, or credit union.

(2) "Check" means a draft, other than a documentary draft, payable on demand and drawn on a bank, even though it is described by another term, such as "share draft" or "negotiable order of withdrawal."

(b) In any dispute concerning payment by means of a check, a duplicate of the check produced in accordance with Code Section 24-10-1003, together with the original bank statement that reflects payment of the check by the bank on which it was drawn or a duplicate thereof produced in the same manner, shall create a presumption that the check has been paid.

§ 24-14-26. Estoppels defined; enumeration generally

(a) Conclusive presumptions of law are termed estoppels; averments to the contrary of such presumptions shall not be allowed. Estoppels are not generally favored.

(b) Estoppels include presumptions in favor of:

(1) A record or judgment unreversed;

(2) The proper conduct of courts and judicial officers acting within their legitimate spheres;

(3) The proper conduct of other officers of the law after the lapse of time has rendered it dangerous to open the investigation of their acts in regard to mere formalities of the law;

(4) Ancient deeds and other instruments more than 30 years old, when they come from proper custody and possession has been held in accordance with them;

(5) Recitals in deeds, except payment of purchase money, as against a grantor, sui juris, acting in his or her own right, and his or her privies in estate, in blood, and in law;

(6) A landlord's title as against his or her tenant in possession;

(7) Solemn admissions made in judicio; or

(8) Admissions upon which other parties have acted, either to their own injury or to the benefit of the persons making the admissions.

Estoppels also include all similar cases where it would be more unjust and productive of evil to hear the truth than to forbear investigation.

§ 24-14-27. Estoppel relating to real estate

(a) Where an estoppel relates to the title to real estate, the party claiming to have been influenced by the other party's acts or declarations shall not only have been ignorant of the true title, but also ignorant of any convenient means of acquiring such knowledge.

(b) Where both parties have equal knowledge or equal means of obtaining the truth, there shall be no estoppel.

§ 24-14-28. Trustees estopped to set up title adverse to trust

Trustees and other representatives with custody of papers have ample opportunities to discover defects in the title of property in their care and shall be estopped from setting up title adverse to their trust.

§ 24-14-29. Equitable estoppel

In order for an equitable estoppel to arise, there shall generally be some intended deception in the conduct or declarations of the party to be estopped, or such gross negligence as to amount to constructive fraud, by which another has been misled to his or her injury.

ARTICLE 3. PARTICULAR MATTERS OF PROOF

§ 24-14-40. Evidence of identity; burden in civil proceedings

(a) Concordance of name alone is some evidence of identity. Residence, vocation, ownership of property, and other like facts may be proved. Reasonable certainty shall be all that is be required.
(b) In civil proceedings, parties shall generally be relieved from the onus of proving identity, as it is a fact generally more easily disproved than established.

§ 24-14-41. Proof of de facto officer

An officer de facto may be proved to be such by his or her acts, without the production of his or her commission or appointment.

§ 24-14-42. Judgment admissible; effect

A judgment shall be admissible between any parties to show the fact of the rendition thereof; between parties and privies it is conclusive as to the matter directly in issue, until reversed or set aside.

§ 24-14-43. Calendars as proof of dates

Stern's United States calendar and Stafford's office calendar shall be admissible in proof of dates for the space of time covered by them respectively without further proof.

§ 24-14-44. American Experience Mortality Tables

In all civil proceedings where the life expectancy of a person shall be an issue, the American Experience Mortality Tables shall be admissible as evidence of the life expectancy of such person.

§ 24-14-45. Other mortality tables

(a) In addition to any other lawful methods of computing the value of the life of a decedent in wrongful death cases or of determining the present value of future due earnings or amounts in proceedings involving permanent personal injuries, there shall be admissible in evidence, as competent evidence in such proceedings, either or both of the following mortality tables:
   (1) The Commissioners 1958 Standard Ordinary Mortality Table; or
   (2) Annuity Mortality Table for 1949, Ultimate.

(b) In addition to the provisions set out in subsection (a) of this Code section, the jury or court shall be authorized in cases of wrongful death or permanent personal injuries to use any table determined by the jury or court, whichever is the trier of fact, to be accurate in showing the value of annuities on single lives according to the mortality tables listed in subsection (a) of this Code section.

(c) The admissible evidence provided for in subsections (a) and (b) of this Code section shall not be the exclusive method which the jury or court is required to use in such proceedings but shall be supplementary to other lawful and allowable evidence and methods for such purpose.

§ 24-14-46. United States Department of Agriculture inspection certificates prima-facie evidence

All inspection certificates issued by the United States Department of Agriculture over the signature of any inspector thereof which are admissible in courts of the United States as prima-facie evidence of the truth of the statements therein contained shall be admissible in all courts of the State of Georgia as prima-facie evidence of the truth of the statements therein contained.

§ 24-14-47. Proof that person is dead or missing as evidence

(a) A written finding of presumed death made by officers or employees of the United States authorized to make such findings pursuant to any law of the United States or a duly certified copy of such finding shall be received in any court, office, or other place in this state as evidence of the death of the person therein found to be dead and the date, circumstances, and place of his or her disappearance.

(b) An official written report, record, or duly certified copy thereof that a person is missing, missing in action, interned in a neutral country, beleaguered, besieged, or captured by an enemy, dead or alive, made by an officer or employee of the United States authorized by any law of the United States to make the same shall be received in any court, office, or other place in this state as evidence that such person is missing, missing in action, interned in a neutral country, beleaguered, besieged, or captured by an enemy, dead or alive, as the case may be.

(c) For the purposes of subsections (a) and (b) of this Code section, any finding, report, record, or duly certified copy thereof purporting to have been signed by an officer or employee of the United States as is described in this Code section shall prima facie be deemed to have been signed and issued by such an officer or employee pursuant to law, and the person signing same shall prima facie be deemed to have acted within the scope of his or her authority.

APPENDIX

AMERICAN EXPERIENCE MORTALITY TABLE

Age	Expectation of Life (Years)
10	48.72
11	48.08
12	47.45
13	46.80
14	46.16
15	45.50
16	44.85
17	44.19
18	43.53
19	42.87
20	42.20
21	41.53
22	40.85
23	40.17
24	39.49
25	38.81
26	38.12
27	37.43
28	36.73
29	36.03
30	35.33
31	34.63
32	33.92
33	33.21
34	32.50
35	31.78
36	31.07
37	30.35
38	29.62
39	28.90
40	28.18

41	27.45
42	26.72
43	26.00
44	25.27
45	24.54
46	23.81
47	23.08
48	22.36
49	21.63
50	20.91
51	20.20
52	19.49
53	18.79
54	18.09
55	17.40
56	16.72
57	16.05
58	15.39
59	14.74
60	14.10
61	13.47
62	12.86
63	12.26
64	11.67
65	11.10
66	10.54
67	10.00
68	9.47
69	8.97
70	8.48
71	8.00
72	7.55
73	7.11
74	6.68
75	6.27
76	5.88
77	5.49
78	5.11
79	4.74
80	4.39
81	4.05
82	3.71
83	3.39
84	3.08
85	2.77
86	2.47

87	2.18
88	1.91
89	1.66
90	1.42
91	1.19
92	.98
93	.80
94	.64
95	.50

THE COMMISSIONERS 1958 STANDARD ORDINARY
MORTALITY TABLE

Age	Expectation of Life (Years)
0	68.30
1	67.78
2	66.90
3	66.00
4	65.10
5	64.19
6	63.27
7	62.35
8	61.43
9	60.51
10	59.58
11	58.65
12	57.72
13	56.80
14	55.87
15	54.95
16	54.03
17	53.11
18	52.19
19	51.28
20	50.37
21	49.46
22	48.55
23	47.64
24	46.73
25	45.82
26	44.90
27	43.99
28	43.08
29	42.16

,

30	41.25
31	40.34
32	39.43
33	38.51
34	37.60
35	36.69
36	35.78
37	34.88
38	33.97
39	33.07
40	32.18
41	31.29
42	30.41
43	29.54
44	28.67
45	27.81
46	26.95
47	26.11
48	25.27
49	24.45
50	23.63
51	22.82
52	22.03
53	21.25
54	20.47
55	19.71
56	18.97
57	18.23
58	17.51
59	16.81
60	16.12
61	15.44
62	14.78
63	14.14
64	13.51
65	12.90
66	12.31
67	11.73
68	11.17
69	10.64
70	10.12
71	9.63
72	9.15
73	8.69
74	8.24
75	7.81

76	7.39
77	6.98
78	6.59
79	6.21
80	5.85
81	5.51
82	5.19
83	4.89
84	4.60
85	4.32
86	4.06
87	3.80
88	3.55
89	3.31
90	3.06
91	2.82
92	2.58
93	2.33
94	2.07
95	1.80
96	1.51
97	1.18
98	.83
99	.50

ANNUITY MORTALITY TABLE FOR 1949, ULTIMATE

Expectation of
Life (Years)

Age	Male	Female
0	73.18	78.69
1	72.47	77.94
2	71.59	77.04
3	70.65	76.10
4	69.70	75.14
5	68.75	74.17
6	67.78	73.19
7	66.82	72.21
8	65.85	71.23
9	64.89	70.24
10	63.92	69.26
11	62.95	68.27
12	61.98	67.29
13	61.01	66.30

14	60.04	65.32
15	59.07	64.33
16	58.10	63.35
17	57.13	62.37
18	56.17	61.39
19	55.20	60.41
20	54.23	59.43
21	53.26	58.45
22	52.30	57.48
23	51.33	56.50
24	50.37	55.53
25	49.41	54.55
26	48.44	53.58
27	47.48	52.61
28	46.52	51.64
29	45.56	50.67
30	44.61	49.70
31	43.65	48.73
32	42.70	47.77
33	41.74	46.80
34	40.79	45.84
35	39.85	44.88
36	38.90	43.92
37	37.96	42.97
38	37.02	42.01
39	36.08	41.06
40	35.15	40.11
41	34.22	39.17
42	33.29	38.22
43	32.38	37.28
44	31.47	36.35
45	30.57	35.41
46	29.67	34.48
47	28.80	33.56
48	27.93	32.64
49	27.07	31.72
50	26.23	30.81
51	25.40	29.91
52	24.58	29.01
53	23.78	28.11
54	22.98	27.22
55	22.20	26.33
56	21.44	25.46
57	20.68	24.59
58	19.93	23.72
59	19.20	22.87

60	18.48	22.02
61	17.76	21.18
62	17.06	20.36
63	16.37	19.54
64	15.68	18.73
65	15.01	17.94
66	14.36	17.16
67	13.71	16.39
68	13.08	15.64
69	12.46	14.90
70	11.86	14.18
71	11.28	13.47
72	10.71	12.78
73	10.15	12.11
74	9.61	11.45
75	9.09	10.82
76	8.58	10.20
77	8.10	9.60
78	7.63	9.02
79	7.17	8.47
80	6.74	7.93
81	6.32	7.42
82	5.92	6.93
83	5.54	6.46
84	5.18	6.01
85	4.84	5.58
86	4.51	5.18
87	4.20	4.79
88	3.90	4.43
89	3.62	4.09
90	3.36	3.77
91	3.12	3.47
92	2.88	3.19
93	2.67	2.92
94	2.47	2.68
95	2.28	2.45
96	2.10	2.24
97	1.94	2.05
98	1.79	1.87
99	1.65	1.71
100	1.52	1.56
101	1.40	1.42
102	1.29	1.30
103	1.20	1.19
104	1.10	1.09
105	1.02	0.99

106	0.94	0.91
107	0.86	0.83
108	0.75	0.73
109	0.50	0.50

Made in the USA
Columbia, SC
27 April 2021